THE BOOK
OF HERMETICA

THE BOOK OF HERMETICA

THE THREE ESSENTIAL TEXTS:

THE CORPUS HERMETICUM,

THE EMERALD TABLET,

THE KYBALION

HERMES TRISMEGISTUS
AND THE THREE INITIATES

ST. MARTIN'S
ESSENTIALS
NEW YORK

Published in the United States by St. Martin's Essentials,
an imprint of St. Martin's Publishing Group

PUBLISHER'S PREFACE. Copyright © 2024 by Joel Fotinos.

www.stmartins.com

Library of Congress Cataloging-in-Publication Data
is available upon request.

ISBN 978-1-250-89784-8 (trade paperback)
ISBN 978-1-250-89785-5 (ebook)

Our books may be purchased in bulk for promotional, educational, or business use. Please contact your local bookseller or the Macmillan Corporate
and Premium Sales Department at 1-800-221-7945, extension 5442, or by
email at MacmillanSpecialMarkets@macmillan.com.

The Corpus Hermeticum was first published in 1471.
The text of *The Emerald Tablet* first appeared in the late
eighth or early ninth century.
The Kybalion was first published in in 1908 by The Yogi Publication Society.

First St. Martin's Essentials Edition: 2024

10   9   8   7   6   5   4

This edition seeks to faithfully reproduce the original publications of the
author's works and so has maintained the original spelling and grammar
throughout, with only minor alterations for clarity or content.

Contents

Publisher's Preface

You hold in your hands the compilation of the three most critical texts of Hermetic wisdom—*Corpus Hermeticum, The Emerald Tablet,* and *The Kybalion.* Together, they compose the three pillars of Hermetic thought as we understand it today.

Hermetic wisdom arose out of the Greco-Egyptian culture spanning from around 300 BCE to 400 AD, and is attributed to a mythical figure called Hermes Trismegistos ("Hermes the Thrice-Greatest"). This figure derives from the Egyptian god Thoth and the Greek god Hermes, both of whom were considered patrons of the writing-centered arts.

The first of the works contained in this volume is the *Corpus Hermeticum,* which many consider to be the core document of the Hermetic tradition, and dates from the early Christian era. It arose from Hellenic Egypt and, like most Hermetic wisdom, is attributed to Hermes Trismegistos. These texts explore philosophy, religion, magic, and alchemy, and are considered the foundation for later alchemical and hermetic thought.

The second text in this collection, *The Emerald Tablet* is also attributed to Hermes Trismegistus, and is believed to have been written between 103 BCE. There is much speculation as to where the text truly originated. According to sources, it first appeared in the West as a part of *Secretum Secretorum*, which was a set of principles that are thought to be written by some of history's greatest thinkers, including Aristotle to Alexander the Great.

The Emerald Tablet is a series of fourteen stanzas, and this edition contains translations from various different iterations of the Tablet, including from the German, Latin, Arabic, Phoenician, Chaldean, Chinese, and French.

Some historians feel that the term "emerald tablet" comes either from the emerald table of the Gothic kings of Spain, or the *Sacro catino*—a dish made of green glass said to have belonged to the Queen of Sheba and been used at the Last Supper.

The final text in this collection is *The Kybalion*, which is more contemporary than the other two texts, and serves as a distillation based on those two primary sources. *The Kybalion* is now widely believed to have been written by William Walker Atkinson, a popular New Thought teacher, under the pseudonym "The Three Initiates" in the early twentieth century.

The Book of Hermetica contains widely accepted texts of these three esoteric writings, which have inspired great minds throughout the ages. It is the perfect introduction to the mysteries of hermeticism and essential reading for anyone interested in understanding Western mythical thought through the ages.

THE CORPUS HERMETICUM

Contents

THE CORPUS HERMETICUM

The Corpus Hermeticum are the core documents of the Hermetic tradition. Dating from early in the Christian era, they were mistakenly dated to a much earlier period by Church officials (and everyone else) up until the 15th century. Because of this, they were allowed to survive and were seen as an early precursor to what was to be Christianity. We know today that they were, in fact, from the early Christian era, and came out of the turbulent religious seas of Hellenic Egypt.

These are all taken from Mead's translations, which are in the public domain at this point.

I. Poemandres, the Shepherd of Men

1. It chanced once on a time my mind was meditating on the things that are, my thought was raised to a great height, the senses of my body being held back—just as men who are weighed down with sleep after a fill of food, or from fatigue of body.

    Methought a Being more than vast, in size beyond all bounds, called out my name and saith: What wouldst thou hear and see, and what hast thou in mind to learn and know?

2. And I do say: Who art thou?

    He saith: I am Man-Shepherd (Poemandres), Mind of all-masterhood; I know what thou desirest and I'm with thee everywhere.

3. [And] I reply: I long to learn the things that are, and comprehend their nature, and know God. This is, I said, what I desire to hear.

    He answered back to me: Hold in thy mind all thou wouldst know, and I will teach thee.

4. E'en with these words His aspect changed, and straightway, in the twinkling of an eye, all things were opened to me, and I see a Vision limitless, all things turned into Light—sweet, joyous [Light]. And I became transported as I gazed.

    But in a little while Darkness came settling down on part [of it], awesome and gloomy, coiling in sinuous folds, so that methought it like unto a snake.

    And then the Darkness changed into some sort of a Moist Nature, tossed about beyond all power of words, belching out smoke as from a fire, and groaning forth a wailing sound that beggars all description.

    [And] after that an outcry inarticulate came forth from it, as though it were a Voice of Fire.

5. [Thereon] out of the Light [...] a Holy Word (Logos) descended on that Nature. And upwards to the height from the Moist Nature leaped forth pure Fire; light was it, swift and active too.

    The Air, too, being light, followed after the Fire; from out of the Earth-and-Water rising up to Fire so that it seemed to hang therefrom.

    But Earth-and-Water stayed so mingled with each other,

that Earth from Water no one could discern. Yet were they moved to hear by reason of the Spirit-Word (Logos) pervading them.

6. Then saith to me Man-Shepherd: Didst understand this Vision what it means?

Nay; that shall I know, said I.

That Light, He said, am I, thy God, Mind, prior to Moist Nature which appeared from Darkness; the Light-Word (Logos) [that appeared] from Mind is Son of God.

What then?—say I.

Know that what sees in thee and hears is the Lord's Word (Logos); but Mind is Father-God. Not separate are they the one from other; just in their union [rather] is it Life consists.

Thanks be to Thee, I said.

So, understand the Light [He answered], and make friends with it.

7. And speaking thus He gazed for long into my eyes, so that I trembled at the look of him.

But when He raised His head, I see in Mind the Light, [but] now in Powers no man could number, and Cosmos grown beyond all bounds, and that the Fire was compassed round about by a most mighty Power, and [now] subdued had come unto a stand.

And when I saw these things I understood by reason of Man-Shepherd's Word (Logos).

8. But as I was in great astonishment, He saith to me again: Thou didst behold in Mind the Archetypal Form whose being is before beginning without end. Thus spake to me Man-Shepherd.

And I say: Whence then have Nature's elements their being?

To this He answer gives: From Will of God. [Nature] received the Word (Logos), and gazing upon the Cosmos Beautiful did copy it, making herself into a cosmos, by means of her own elements and by the births of souls.

9. And God-the-Mind, being male and female both, as Light and Life subsisting, brought forth another Mind to give things form, who, God as he was of Fire and Spirit, formed Seven Rulers who enclose the cosmos that the sense perceives. Men call their ruling Fate.

10. Straightway from out the downward elements God's Reason (Logos) leaped up to Nature's pure formation, and was at-oned with the Formative Mind; for it was co-essential with it. And Nature's downward elements were thus left reasonless, so as to be pure matter.

11. Then the Formative Mind ([at-oned] with Reason), he who surrounds the spheres and spins them with his whorl, set turning his formations, and let them turn from a beginning boundless unto an endless end. For that the circulation of these [spheres] begins where it doth end, as Mind doth will.

And from the downward elements Nature brought forth lives reason-less; for He did not extend the Reason (Logos) [to them]. The Air brought forth things winged; the Water things that swim, and Earth-and-Water one from another parted, as Mind willed. And from her bosom Earth produced what lives she had, four-footed things and reptiles, beasts wild and tame.

12. But All-Father Mind, being Life and Light, did bring forth Man co-equal to Himself, with whom He fell in love, as being His own child; for he was beautiful beyond compare, the

Image of his Sire. In very truth, God fell in love with his own Form; and on him did bestow all of His own formations.

13. And when he gazed upon what the Enformer had created in the Father, [Man] too wished to enform; and [so] assent was given him by the Father.

Changing his state to the formative sphere, in that he was to have his whole authority, he gazed upon his Brother's creatures. They fell in love with him, and gave him each a share of his own ordering.

And after that he had well learned their essence and had become a sharer in their nature, he had a mind to break right through the Boundary of their spheres, and to subdue the might of that which pressed upon the Fire.

14. So he who hath the whole authority o'er [all] the mortals in the cosmos and o'er its lives irrational, bent his face downwards through the Harmony, breaking right through its strength, and showed to downward Nature God's fair form.

And when she saw that Form of beauty which can never satiate, and him who [now] possessed within himself each single energy of [all seven] Rulers as well as God's own Form, she smiled with love; for 'twas as though she'd seen the image of Man's fairest form upon her Water, his shadow on her Earth.

He in turn beholding the form like to himself, existing in her, in her Water, loved it and willed to live in it; and with the will came act, and [so] he vivified the form devoid of reason.

And Nature took the object of her love and wound herself completely around him, and they were intermingled, for they were lovers.

15. And this is why beyond all creatures on the earth man is
    twofold; mortal because of body, but because of the essential
    man immortal.

    Though deathless and possessed of sway o'er all, yet doth
    he suffer as a mortal doth, subject to Fate.

    Thus though above the Harmony, within the Harmony he
    hath become a slave. Though male-female, as from a Father
    male-female, and though he's sleepless from a sleepless [Sire],
    yet is he overcome [by sleep].

16. Thereon [I say: Teach on], O Mind of me, for I myself as well
    am amorous of the Word (Logos).

    The Shepherd said: This is the mystery kept hid until
    this day.

    Nature embraced by Man brought forth a wonder, oh so
    wonderful. For as he had the nature of the Concord of the
    Seven, who, as I said to thee, [were made] of Fire and Spirit—
    Nature delayed not, but immediately brought forth seven
    "men", in correspondence with the natures of the Seven,
    male-female and moving in the air.

    Thereon [I said]: O Shepherd, . . . , for now I'm filled
    with great desire and long to hear; do not run off.

    The Shepherd said: Keep silence, for not as yet have I
    unrolled for thee the first discourse (logoi).

    Lo! I am still, I said.

17. In such wise than, as I have said, the generation of these
    seven came to pass. Earth was as woman, her Water filled
    with longing; ripeness she took from Fire, spirit from Aether.
    Nature thus brought forth frames to suit the form of Man.

    And Man from Light and Life changed into soul and
    mind—from Life to soul, from Light to mind.

And thus continued all the sense-world's parts until the period of their end and new beginnings.

18. Now listen to the rest of the discourse (Logos) which thou dost long to hear.

The period being ended, the bond that bound them all was loosened by God's Will. For all the animals being male-female, at the same time with Man were loosed apart; some became partly male, some in like fashion [partly] female. And straightway God spake by His Holy Word (Logos):

"Increase ye in increasing, and multiply in multitude, ye creatures and creations all; and man that hath Mind in him, let him learn to know that he himself is deathless, and that the cause of death is love, though Love is all."

19. When He said this, His Forethought did by means of Fate and Harmony effect their couplings and their generations founded. And so all things were multiplied according to their kind.

And he who thus hath learned to know himself, hath reached that Good which doth transcend abundance; but he who through a love that leads astray, expends his love upon his body—he stays in Darkness wandering, and suffering through his senses things of Death.

20. What is the so great fault, said I, the ignorant commit, that they should be deprived of deathlessness?

Thou seem'st, He said, O thou, not to have given heed to what thou heardest. Did I not bid thee think?

Yea do I think, and I remember, and therefore give Thee thanks.

If thou didst think [thereon], [said He], tell me: Why do they merit death who are in Death?

It is because the gloomy Darkness is the root and base of the material frame; from it came the Moist Nature; from this the body in the sense-world was composed; and from this [body] Death doth the Water drain.

21. Right was thy thought, O thou! But how doth "he who knows himself, go unto Him", as God's Word (Logos) hath declared?

And I reply: the Father of the universals doth consist of Light and Life, from Him Man was born.

Thou sayest well, [thus] speaking. Light and Life is Father-God, and from Him Man was born.

If then thou learnest that thou art thyself of Life and Light, and that thou [happen'st] to be out of them, thou shalt return again to Life. Thus did Man-Shepherd speak.

But tell me further, Mind of me, I cried, how shall I come to Life again . . . for God doth say: "The man who hath Mind in him, let him learn to know that he himself [is deathless]."

22. Have not all men then Mind?

Thou sayest well, O thou, thus speaking. I, Mind, myself am present with holy men and good, the pure and merciful, men who live piously.

[To such] my presence doth become an aid, and straight-way they gain gnosis of all things, and win the Father's love by their pure lives, and give Him thanks, invoking on Him blessings, and chanting hymns, intent on Him with ardent love.

And ere they give up the body unto its proper death, they turn them with disgust from its sensations, from knowledge of what things they operate. Nay, it is I, the Mind, that will not let the operations which befall the body, work to their [natural] end. For being door-keeper I'll close up [all] the entrances, and cut the mental actions off which base and evil energies induce.

23. But to the Mind-less ones, the wicked and depraved, the envious and covetous, and those who mured do and love impiety, I am far off, yielding my place to the Avenging Daimon, who sharpening the fire, tormenteth him and addeth fire to fire upon him, and rusheth upon him through his senses, thus rendering him readier for transgressions of the law, so that he meets with greater torment; nor doth he ever cease to have desire for appetites inordinate, insatiately striving in the dark.

24. Well hast thou taught me all, as I desired, O Mind. And now, pray, tell me further of the nature of the Way Above as now it is [for me].

To this Man-Shepherd said: When the material body is to be dissolved, first thou surrenderest the body by itself unto the work of change, and thus the form thou hadst doth vanish, and thou surrenderest thy way of life, void of its energy, unto the Daimon. The body's senses next pass back into their sources, becoming separate, and resurrect as energies; and passion and desire withdraw unto that nature which is void of reason.

25. And thus it is that man doth speed his way thereafter upwards through the Harmony.

To the first zone he gives the Energy of Growth and Waning; unto the second [zone], Device of Evils [now] de-energized; unto the third, the Guile of the Desires de-energized; unto the fourth, his Domineering Arrogance, [also] de-energized; unto the fifth, unholy Daring and the Rashness of Audacity, de-energized; unto the sixth, Striving for Wealth by evil means, deprived of its aggrandizement; and to the seventh zone, Ensnaring Falsehood, de-energized.

26. And then, with all the energisings of the harmony stript from him, clothed in his proper Power, he cometh to that Nature which belongs unto the Eighth, and there with those-that-are hymneth the Father.

They who are there welcome his coming there with joy; and he, made like to them that sojourn there, doth further hear the Powers who are above the Nature that belongs unto the Eighth, singing their songs of praise to God in language of their own.

And then they, in a band, go to the Father home; of their own selves they make surrender of themselves to Powers, and [thus] becoming Powers they are in God. This the good end for those who have gained Gnosis—to be made one with God.

Why shouldst thou then delay? Must it not be, since thou hast all received, that thou shouldst to the worthy point the way, in order that through thee the race of mortal kind may by [thy] God be saved?

27. This when He'd said, Man-Shepherd mingled with the Powers.

But I, with thanks and belssings unto the Father of the universal [Powers], was freed, full of the power he had poured into me, and full of what He'd taught me of the nature of the All and of the loftiest Vision.

And I began to preach unto men the Beauty of Devotion and of Gnosis:

O ye people, earth-born folk, ye who have given yourselves to drunkenness and sleep and ignorance of God, be sober now, cease from your surfeit, cease to be glamoured by irrational sleep!

28. And when they heard, they came with one accord. Whereon I say:

Ye earth-born folk, why have ye given yourselves up to Death, while yet ye have the power of sharing Deathlessness? Repent, O ye, who walk with Error arm in arm and make of Ignorance the sharer of your board; get ye out from the light of Darkness, and take your part in Deathlessness, forsake Destruction!

29. And some of them with jests upon their lips departed [from me], abandoning themselves unto the Way of Death; others entreated to be taught, casting themselves before my feet.

But I made them arise, and I became a leader of the Race towards home, teaching the words (logoi), how and in what way they shall be saved. I sowed in them the words (logoi) of wisdom; of Deathless Water were they given to drink.

And when even was come and all sun's beams began to set, I bade them all give thanks to God. And when they had brought to an end the giving of their thanks, each man returned to his own resting place.

30. But I recorded in my heart Man-Shepherd's benefaction, and with my every hope fulfilled more than rejoiced. For body's sleep became the soul's awakening, and closing of the eyes— true vision, pregnant with Good my silence, and the utterance of my word (logos) begetting of good things.

All this befell me from my Mind, that is Man-Shepherd, Word (Logos) of all masterhood, by whom being God-inspired

I came unto the Plain of Truth. Wherefore with all my soul and strength thanksgiving give I unto Father-God.

31. Holy art Thou, O God, the universals' Father.

Holy art Thou, O God, whose Will perfects itself by means of its own Powers.

Holy art Thou, O God, who willeth to be known and art known by Thine own.

Holy art Thou, who didst by Word (Logos) make to consist the things that are.

Holy art Thou, of whom All-nature hath been made an image.

Holy art Thou, whose Form Nature hath never made.

Holy art Thou, more powerful than all power.

Holy art Thou, transcending all pre-eminence.

Holy Thou art, Thou better than all praise.

Accept my reason's offerings pure, from soul and heart for aye stretched up to Thee, O Thou unutterable, unspeakable, Whose Name naught but the Silence can express.

32. Give ear to me who pray that I may ne'er of Gnosis fail, [Gnosis] which is our common being's nature; and fill me with Thy Power, and with this Grace [of Thine], that I may give the Light to those in ignorance of the Race, my Brethren, and Thy Sons.

For this cause I believe, and I bear witness; I go to Life and Light. Blessed art Thou, O Father. Thy Man would holy be as Thou art holy, e'en as Thou gave him Thy full authority [to be].

II. To Asclepius

1. Hermes: All that is moved, Asclepius, is it not moved in something and by something?

    Asclepius: Assuredly.

    H: And must not that in which it's moved be greater than the moved?

    A: It must.

    H: Mover, again, has greater power than moved?

    A: It has, of course.

    H: The nature, furthermore, of that in which it's moved must be quite other from the nature of the moved?

    A: It must completely.

2. H: Is not, again, this cosmos vast, [so vast] that than it there exists no body greater?

    A: Assuredly.

    H: And massive, too, for it is crammed with multitudes of other mighty frames, nay, rather all the other bodies that there are?

    A: It is.

    H: And yet the cosmos is a body?

    A: It is a body.

    H: And one that's moved?

3. A: Assuredly.

    H: Of what size, then, must be the space in which it's moved, and of what kind [must be] the nature [of that space]? Must it not be far vaster [than the cosmos], in order that it may be able to find room for its continued course, so that the moved may not be cramped for want of room and lose its motion?

A: Something, Thrice-greatest one, it needs must be, immensely vast.

4. H: And of what nature? Must it not be, Asclepius, of just the contrary? And is not contrary to body bodiless?

A: Agreed.

H: Space, then, is bodiless. But bodiless must either be some godlike thing or God [Himself]. And by "some godlike thing" I mean no more the generable [i.e., that which is generated] but the ingenerable.

5. If, then, space be some godlike thing, it is substantial; but if 'tis God [Himself], it transcends substance. But it is to be thought of otherwise [than God], and in this way.

God is first "thinkable" for us, not for Himself, for that the thing that's thought doth fall beneath the thinker's sense. God then cannot be "thinkable" unto Himself, in that He's thought of by Himself as being nothing else but what He thinks. But he is "something else" for us, and so He's thought of by us.

6. If space is, therefore, to be thought, [it should] not, [then, be thought as] God, but space. If God is also to be thought, [He should] not [be conceived] as space, but as energy that can contain [all space].

Further, all that is moved is moved not in the moved but in the stable. And that which moves [another] is of course stationary, for 'tis impossible that it should move with it.

A: How is it, then, that things down here, Thrice-greatest one, are moved with those that are [already] moved? For thou hast said the errant spheres were moved by the inerrant one.

H: This is not, O Asclepius, a moving with, but one against; they are not moved with one another, but one against the other. It is this contrariety which turneth the resistance of their motion into rest. For that resistance is the rest of motion.

7. Hence, too, the errant spheres, being moved contrarily to the inerrant one, are moved by one another by mutual contrariety, [and also] by the stable one through contrariety itself. And this can otherwise not be.

The Bears up there, which neither set nor rise, think'st thou they rest or move?

A: They move, Thrice-greatest one.

H: And what their motion, my Asclepius?

A: Motion that turns for ever round the same.

H: But revolution—motion around same—is fixed by rest. For "round-the-same" doth stop "beyond-same". "Beyond-same" then, being stopped, if it be steadied in "round-same"—the contrary stands firm, being rendered ever stable by its contrariety.

8. Of this I'll give thee here on earth an instance, which the eye can see. Regard the animals down here—a man, for instance, swimming! The water moves, yet the resistance of his hands and feet give him stability, so that he is not borne along with it, nor sunk thereby.

A: Thou hast, Thrice-greatest one, adduced a most clear instance.

H: All motion, then, is caused in station and by station.

The motion, therefore, of the cosmos (and of every other hylic animal) will not be caused by things exterior to the cosmos, but by things interior [outward] to the exterior—such [things] as soul, or spirit, or some such other thing incorporeal.

'Tis not the body that doth move the living thing in it;
nay, not even the whole [body of the universe a lesser] body
e'en though there be no life in it.

9. A: What meanest thou by this, Thrice-greatest one? Is it not
bodies, then, that move the stock and stone and all the other
things inanimate?

H: By no means, O Asclepius. The something-in-the-
body, the that-which-moves the thing inanimate, this surely's
not a body, for that it moves the two of them—both body of
the lifter and the lifted? So that a thing that's lifeless will not
move a lifeless thing. That which doth move [another thing]
is animate, in that it is the mover.

Thou seest, then, how heavy laden is the soul, for it alone
doth lift two bodies. That things, moreover, moved are moved
in something as well as moved by something is clear.

10. A: Yea, O Thrice-greatest one, things moved must needs be
moved in something void.

H: Thou sayest well, O [my] Asclepius! For naught
of things that are is void. Alone the "is-not" is void [and]
stranger to subsistence. For that which is subsistent can never
change to void.

A: Are there, then, O Thrice-greatest one, no such things
as an empty cask, for instance, and an empty jar, a cup and vat,
and other things like unto them?

H: Alack, Asclepius, for thy far-wandering from the truth!
Think'st thou that things most full and most replete are void?

11. A: How meanest thou, Thrice-greatest one?

H: Is not air body?

A: It is.

H: And doth this body not pervade all things, and so, pervading, fill them? And "body"; doth body not consist from blending of the "four"? Full, then, of air are all thou callest void; and if of air, then of the "four".

Further, of this the converse follows, that all thou callest full are void—of air; for that they have their space filled out with other bodies, and, therefore, are not able to receive the air therein. These, then, which thou dost say are void, they should be hollow named, not void; for they not only are, but they are full of air and spirit.

12. A: Thy argument (logos), Thrice-greatest one, is not to be gainsaid; air is a body. Further, it is this body which doth pervade all things, and so, pervading, fill them. What are we, then, to call that space in which the all doth move?

H: The bodiless, Asclepius.

A: What, then, is Bodiless?

H: 'Tis Mind and Reason (logos), whole out of whole, all self-embracing, free from all body, from all error free, unsensible to body and untouchable, self stayed in self, containing all, preserving those that are, whose rays, to use a likeness, are Good, Truth, Light beyond light, the Archetype of soul.

A: What, then, is God?

13. H: Not any one of these is He; for He it is that causeth them to be, both all and each and every thing of all that are. Nor hath He left a thing beside that is-not; but they are all from things-that-are and not from things-that-are-not. For that the things-that-are-not have naturally no power of being anything, but naturally have the power of the inability-to-be. And, conversely, the things-that-are have not the nature of some time not-being.

14. A: What say'st thou ever, then, God is?

    H: God, therefore, is not Mind, but Cause that the Mind is; God is not Spirit, but Cause that Spirit is; God is not Light, but Cause that the Light is. Hence one should honor God with these two names [the Good and Father]—names which pertain to Him alone and no one else.

    For no one of the other so-called gods, no one of men, or daimones, can be in any measure Good, but God alone; and He is Good alone and nothing else. The rest of things are separable all from the Good's nature; for [all the rest] are soul and body, which have no place that can contain the Good.

15. For that as mighty is the Greatness of the Good as is the Being of all things that are—both bodies and things bodiless, things sensible and intelligible things. Call thou not, therefore, aught else Good, for thou would'st impious be; nor anything at all at any time call God but Good alone, for so thou would'st again be impious.

16. Though, then, the Good is spoken of by all, it is not understood by all, what thing it is. Not only, then, is God not understood by all, but both unto the gods and some of the men they out of ignorance do give the name of Good, though they can never either be or become Good. For they are very different from God, while Good can never be distinguished from Him, for that God is the same as Good.

    The rest of the immortal ones are nonetheless honored with the name of God, and spoken of as gods; but God is Good not out of courtesy but out of nature. For that God's nature and the Good is one; one is the kind of both, from which all other kinds [proceed].

The Good is he who gives all things and naught receives. God, then, doth give all things and receive naught. God, then, is Good, and Good is God.

17. The other name of God is Father, again because He is the that-which-maketh-all. The part of father is to make.

Wherefore child-making is a very great and a most pious thing in life for them who think aright, and to leave life on earth without a child a very great misfortune and impiety; and he who hath no child is punished by the daimones after death.

And this is the punishment: that that man's soul who hath no child, shall be condemned unto a body with neither man's nor woman's nature, a thing accursed beneath the sun.

Wherefore, Asclepius, let not your sympathies be with the man who hath no child, but rather pity his mishap, knowing what punishment abides for him.

Let all that has been said then, be to thee, Asclepius, an introduction to the gnosis of the nature of all things.

III. The Sacred Sermon

1. The Glory of all things is God, Godhead and Godly Nature. Source of the things that are is God, who is both Mind and Nature—yea Matter, the Wisdom that reveals all things. Source [too] is Godhead—yea Nature, Energy, Necessity, and End, and Making-new-again.

Darkness that knew no bounds was in Abyss, and Water [too] and subtle Breath intelligent; these were by Power of God in Chaos.

Then Holy Light arose; and there collected 'neath Dry

Space from out Moist Essence Elements; and all the Gods do separate things out from fecund Nature.

2. All things being undefined and yet unwrought, the light things were assigned unto the height, the heavy ones had their foundations laid down underneath the moist part of Dry Space, the universal things being bounded off by Fire and hanged in Breath to keep them up.

And Heaven was seen in seven circles; its Gods were visible in forms of stars with all their signs; while Nature had her members made articulate together with the Gods in her. And [Heaven's] periphery revolved in cyclic course, borne on by Breath of God.

3. And every God by his own proper power brought forth what was appointed him. Thus there arose four-footed beasts, and creeping things, and those that in the water dwell, and things with wings, and everything that beareth seed, and grass, and shoot of every flower, all having in themselves seed of again-becoming.

And they selected out the births of men for gnosis of the works of God and attestation of the energy of Nature; the multitude of men for lordship over all beneath the heaven and gnosis of its blessings, that they might increase in increasing and multiply in multitude, and every soul infleshed by revolution of the Cyclic Gods, for observation of the marvels of Heaven and Heaven's Gods' revolution, and of the works of God and energy of Nature, for tokens of its blessings, for gnosis of the power of God, that they might know the fates that follow good and evil [deeds] and learn the cunning work of all good arts.

4. [Thus] there begins their living and their growing wise,

according to the fate appointed by the revolution of the Cy-clic Gods, and their deceasing for this end.

And there shall be memorials mighty of their handiworks upon the earth, leaving dim trace behind when cycles are renewed.

For every birth of flesh ensouled, and of the fruit of seed, and every handiwork, though it decay, shall of necessity re-new itself, both by the renovation of the Gods and by the turning-round of Nature's rhythmic wheel.

For that whereas the Godhead is Nature's ever-making-new-again the cosmic mixture, Nature herself is also co-established in that Godhead.

IV. The Cup or Monad

1. Hermes: With Reason (Logos), not with hands, did the World-maker make the universal World; so that thou shouldst think of him as everywhere and ever-being, the Author of all things, and One and Only, who by His Will all beings hath created.

    This Body of Him is a thing no man can touch, or see, or measure, a body inextensible, like to no other frame. 'Tis neither Fire nor Water, Air nor Breath; yet all of them come from it. Now being Good he willed to consecrate this [Body] to Himself alone, and set its Earth in order and adorn it.

2. So down [to Earth] He sent the Cosmos of this Frame Divine—man, a life that cannot die, and yet a life that dies. And o'er [all other] lives and over Cosmos [too], did man excel by reason of the Reason (Logos) and the Mind. For contemplator of God's works did man become; he marvelled and did strive to know their Author.

3. Reason (Logos) indeed, O Tat, among all men hath He distributed, but Mind not yet; not that He grudgeth any, for grudging cometh not from Him, but hath its place below, within the souls of men who have no Mind.

    Tat: Why then did God, O father, not on all bestow a share of Mind?

    H: He willed, my son, to have it set up in the midst for souls, just as it were a prize.

4. T: And where hath He set it up?

    H: He filled a mighty Cup with it, and sent it down, joining a Herald [to it], to whom He gave command to make this proclamation to the hearts of men:

    Baptize thyself with this Cup's baptism, what heart can do so, thou that hast faith thou canst ascend to him that hath sent down the Cup, thou that dost know for what thou didst come into being!

    As many then as understood the Herald's tidings and doused themselves in Mind, became partakers in the Gnosis; and when they had "received the Mind" they were made "perfect men".

    But they who do not understand the tidings, these, since they possess the aid of Reason [only] and not Mind, are ignorant wherefor they have come into being and whereby.

5. The senses of such men are like irrational creatures'; and as their [whole] make-up is in their feelings and their impulses, they fail in all appreciation of those things which really are worth contemplation. These center all their thought upon the pleasures of the body and its appetites, in the belief that for its sake man hath come into being.

    But they who have received some portion of God's gift,

these, Tat, if we judge by their deeds, have from Death's bonds won their release; for they embrace in their own Mind all things, things on the earth, things in the heaven, and things above the heaven—if there be aught. And having raised themselves so far they sight the Good; and having sighted it, they look upon their sojourn here as a mischance; and in disdain of all, both things in body and the bodiless, they speed their way unto that One and Only One.

6. This is, O Tat, the Gnosis of the Mind, Vision of things Divine; God-knowledge is it, for the Cup is God's.

   T: Father, I, too, would be baptized.

   H: Unless thou first shall hate thy Body, son, thou canst not love thy Self. But if thou lov'st thy Self thou shalt have Mind, and having Mind thou shalt share in the Gnosis.

   T: Father, what dost thou mean?

   H: It is not possible, my son, to give thyself to both—I mean to things that perish and to things divine. For seeing that existing things are twain, Body and Bodiless, in which the perishing and the divine are understood, the man who hath the will to choose is left the choice of one or the other; for it can never be the twain should meet. And in those souls to whom the choice is left, the waning of the one causes the other's growth to show itself.

7. Now the choosing of the Better not only proves a lot most fair for him who makes the choice, seeing it makes the man a God, but also shows his piety to God. Whereas the [choosing] of the Worse, although it doth destroy the "man", it doth only disturb God's harmony to this extent, that as processions pass by in the middle of the way, without being able to do anything but take the road from others, so do such men

move in procession through the world led by their bodies' pleasures.

8. This being so, O Tat, what comes from God hath been and will be ours; but that which is dependent on ourselves, let this press onward and have no delay, for 'tis not God, 'tis we who are the cause of evil things, preferring them to good.

    Thou see'st, son, how many are the bodies through which we have to pass, how many are the choirs of daimones, how vast the system of the star-courses [through which our Path doth lie], to hasten to the One and Only God.

    For to the Good there is no other shore; It hath no bounds; It is without an end; and for Itself It is without beginning, too, though unto us it seemeth to have one—the Gnosis.

9. Therefore to It Gnosis is no beginning; rather is it [that Gnosis doth afford] to us the first beginning of its being known.

    Let us lay hold, therefore, of the beginning. and quickly speed through all [we have to pass].

    'Tis very hard, to leave the things we have grown used to, which meet our gaze on every side, and turn ourselves back to the Old Old [Path].

    Appearances delight us, whereas things which appear not make their believing hard.

    Now evils are the more apparent things, whereas the Good can never show Itself unto the eyes, for It hath neither form nor figure.

    Therefore the Good is like Itself alone, and unlike all things else; or 'tis impossible that That which hath no body should make Itself apparent to a body.

10. The "Like's" superiority to the "Unlike" and the "Unlike's" inferiority unto the "Like" consists in this:

The Oneness being Source and Root of all, is in all things as Root and Source. Without [this] Source is naught; whereas the Source [Itself] is from naught but itself, since it is Source of all the rest. It is Itself Its Source, since It may have no other Source.

The Oneness then being Source, containeth every number, but is contained by none; engendereth every number, but is engendered by no other one.

11. Now all that is engendered is imperfect, it is divisible, to increase subject and to decrease; but with the Perfect [One] none of these things doth hold. Now that which is increasable increases from the Oneness, but succumbs through its own feebleness when it no longer can contain the One.

And now, O Tat, God's Image hath been sketched for thee, as far as it can be; and if thou wilt attentively dwell on it and observe it with thine heart's eyes, believe me, son, thou'lt find the Path that leads above; nay, that Image shall become thy Guide itself, because the Sight [Divine] hath this peculiar [charm], it holdeth fast and draweth unto it those who succeed in opening their eyes, just as, they say, the magnet [draweth] iron.

V. Though Unmanifest God Is Most Manifest

1. I will recount to thee this sermon (logos) too, O Tat, that thou may'st cease to be without the mysteries of the God beyond all name. And mark thou well how that which to the many seems unmanifest, will grow most manifest for thee.

Now were it manifest, it would not be. For all that is

made manifest is subject to becoming, for it hath been made manifest. But the Unmanifest for ever is, for It doth not desire to be made manifest. It ever is, and maketh manifest all other things.

Being Himself unmanifest, as ever being and ever making-manifest, Himself is not made manifest. God is not made Himself; by thinking-manifest, He thinketh all things manifest.

Now "thinking-manifest" deals with things made alone, for thinking-manifest is nothing else than making.

2.　He, then, alone who is not made, 'tis clear, is both beyond all power of thinking-manifest, and is unmanifest.

And as He thinketh all things manifest, He manifests through all things and in all, and most of all in whatsoever things He wills to manifest.

Do thou, then, Tat, my son, pray first unto our Lord and Father, the One-and-Only One, from whom the One doth come, to show His mercy unto thee, in order that thou mayest have the power to catch a thought of this so mighty God, one single beam of Him to shine into thy thinking. For thought alone "sees" the Unmanifest, in that it is itself unmanifest.

If, then, thou hast the power, He will, Tat, manifest to thy mind's eyes. The Lord begrudgeth not Himself to anything, but manifests Himself through the whole world.

Thou hast the power of taking thought, of seeing it and grasping it in thy own "hands," and gazing face to face upon God's Image. But if what is within thee even is unmanifest to thee, how, then, shall He Himself who is within thy self be manifest for thee by means of [outer] eyes?

3. But if thou wouldst "see" him, bethink thee of the sun, be-
    think thee of moon's course, bethink thee of the order of
    the stars. Who is the One who watcheth o'er that order?
    For every order hath its boundaries marked out by place and
    number.

    The sun's the greatest god of gods in heaven; to whom
    all of the heavenly gods give place as unto king and master.
    And he, this so-great one, he greater than the earth and sea,
    endures to have above him circling smaller stars than him.
    Out of respect to Whom, or out of fear of Whom, my son,
    [doth he do this]?

    Nor like nor equal is the course each of these stars de-
    scribes in heaven. Who [then] is He who marketh out the
    manner of their course and its extent?

4. The Bear up there that turneth round itself, and carries
    round the whole cosmos with it—Who is the owner of this
    instrument? Who He who hath set round the sea its bounds?
    Who He who hath set on its seat the earth?

    For, Tat, there is someone who is the Maker and the Lord
    of all these things. It cound not be that number, place and
    measure could be kept without someone to make them. No
    order whatsoever could be made by that which lacketh place
    and lacketh measure; nay, even this is not without a lord, my
    son. For if the orderless lacks something, in that it is not lord
    of order's path, it also is beneath a lord—the one who hath
    not yet ordained it order.

5. Would that it were possible for thee to get thee wings, and
    soar into the air, and, poised midway 'tween earth and heaven,
    behold the earth's solidity, the sea's fluidity (the flowings of
    its streams), the spaciousness of air, fire's swiftness, [and] the

coursing of the stars, the swiftness of heaven's circuit round them [all]!

Most blessed sight were it, my son, to see all these beneath one sway—the motionless in motion, and the unmanifest made manifest; whereby is made this order of the cosmos and the cosmos which we see of order.

6. If thou would'st see Him too through things that suffer death, both on the earth and in the deep, think of a man's being fashioned in the womb, my son, and strictly scrutinize the art of Him who fashions him, and learn who fashioneth this fair and godly image of the Man.

Who [then] is He who traceth out the circles of the eyes; who He who boreth out the nostrils and the ears; who He who openeth [the portal of] the mouth; who He who doth stretch out and tie the nerves; who He who channels out the veins; who He who hardeneth the bones; who He who covereth the flesh with skin; who He who separates the fingers and the joints; who He who widens out a treading for the feet; who He who diggeth out the ducts; who He who spreadeth out the spleen; who he who shapeth heart like to a pyramid; who He who setteth ribs together; who He who widineth the liver out; who He who maketh lungs like to a sponge; who He who maketh belly stretch so much; who he who doth make prominent the parts most honorable, so that they may be seen, while hiding out of sight those of least honor?

7. Behold how many arts [employed] on one material, how many labors on one single sketch; and all exceeding fair, and all in perfect measure, yet all diversified! Who made them all? What mother, or what sire, save God alone, unmanifest, who hath made all things by His Will?

8. And no one saith a statue or a picture comes to be without a sculptor or [without] a painter; doth [then] such workmanship as this exist without a Worker? What depth of blindness, what deep impiety, what depth of ignorance! See, [then] thou ne'er, son Tat, deprivest works of Worker!

   Nay, rather is He greater than all names, so great is He, the Father of them all. For verily He is the Only One, and this is His work, to be a father.

9. So, if thou forcest me somewhat too bold, to speak, His being is conceiving of all things and making [them].

   And as without its maker it is impossible that anything should be, so ever is He not unless He ever makes all things, in heaven, in air, in earth, in deep, in all of cosmos, in every part that is and that is not of everything. For there is naught in all the world that is not He.

   He is Himself, both things that are and things that are not. The things that are He hath made manifest, He keepeth things that are not in Himself.

10. He is the God beyond all name; He the unmanifest, He the most manifest; He whom the mind [alone] can contemplate, He visible to the eyes [as well]; He is the one of no body, the one of many bodies, nay, rather He of every body.

    Naught is there which he is not. For all are He and He is all. And for this cause hath He all names, in that they are one Father's. And for this cause hath He Himself no nome, in that He's Father of [them] all.

    Who, then, may sing Thee praise of Thee, or [praise] to Thee?

    Whither, again, am I to turn my eyes to sing Thy praise; above, below, within, without?

There is no way, no place [is there] about Thee, nor any other thing of things that are.

All [are] in Thee; all [are] from Thee, O Thou who givest all and takest naught, for Thou hast all and naught is there Thou hast not.

11. And when, O Father, shall I hymn Thee? For none can seize Thy hour or time.

For what, again, shall I sing hymn? For things that Thou hast made, or things Thou hast not? For things Thou hast made manifest, or things Thou hast concealed?

How, further, shall I hymn Thee? As being of myself? As having something of mine own? As being other?

For that Thou art whatever I may be; Thou art whatever I may do; Thou art whatever I may speak.

For Thou art all, and there is nothing else which Thou art not. Thou art all that which doth exist, and Thou art what doth not exist—Mind when Thou thinkest, and Father when Thou makest, and God when Thou dost energize, and Good and Maker of all things.

For that the subtler part of matter is the air, of air the soul, of soul the mind, and of mind God.

VI. In God Alone Is Good and Elsewhere Nowhere

1. Good, O Asclepius, is in none else save in God alone; nay, rather, Good is God Himself eternally.

If it be so, [Good] must be essence, from every kind of motion and becoming free (though naught is free from It), possessed of stable energy around Itself, never too little, nor too much, an ever-full supply. [Though] one, yet [is It] source of all; for what supplieth all is Good. When I, moreover, say [supplieth] altogether [all], it is for ever Good. But this belongs to no one else save God alone.

For He stands not in need of any thing, so that desiring it He should be bad; nor can a single thing of things that are be lost to him, on losing which He should be pained; for pain is part of bad.

Nor is there aught superior to Him, that He should be subdued by it; nor any peer to Him to do Him wrong, or [so that] He should fall in love on its account; nor aught that gives no ear to Him, whereat He should grow angry; nor wiser aught, for Him to envy.

2. Now as all these are non-existent in His being, what is there left but Good alone?

For just as naught of bad is to be found in such transcendent Being, so too in no one of the rest will Good be found.

For in them are all of the other things—both in the little and the great, both in each severally and in this living one that's greater than them all and the mightiest [of them].

For things subject to birth abound in passions, birth in itself being passible. But where there's passion, nowhere is there Good; and where is Good, nowhere a single passion. For where is day, nowhere is night; and where is night, day is nowhere.

Wherefore in genesis the Good can never be, but only be in the ingenerate.

But seeing that the sharing in all things hath been bestowed on matter, so doth it share in Good.

In this way is the Cosmos Good; that, in so far as it doth

make all things, as far as making goes it's Good, but in all other things it is not Good. For it's both passible and subject unto motion, and maker of things passible.

3. Whereas in man by greater or less of bad is good determined. For what is not too bad down here, is good, and good down here is the least part of bad.

    It cannot, therefore, be that good down here should be quite clean of bad, for down here good is fouled with bad; and being fouled, it stays no longer good, and staying not it changes into bad.

    In God alone, is, therefore, Good, or rather Good is God Himself.

    So then, Asclepius, the name alone of Good is found in men, the thing itself nowhere [in them], for this can never be.

    For no material body doth contain It—a thing bound on all sides by bad, by labors, pains, desires and passions, by error and by foolish thoughts.

    And greatest ill of all, Asclepius, is that each of these things that have been said above, is thought down here to be the greatest good.

    And what is still an even greater ill, is belly-lust, the error that doth lead the band of all the other ills—the thing that makes us turn down here from Good.

4. And I, for my part, give thanks to God, that He hath cast it in my mind about the Gnosis of the Good, that it can never be It should be in the world. For that the world is "fullness" of the bad, but God of Good, and Good of God.

    The excellencies of the Beautiful are round the very essence [of the Good]; nay, they do seem too pure, too unalloyed; perchance 'tis they that are themselves Its essences.

For one may dare to say, Asclepius—if essence, sooth, He have—God's essence is the Beautiful; the Beautiful is further also Good.

There is no Good that can be got from objects in the world. For all the things that fall beneath the eye are image-things and pictures as it were; while those that do not meet [the eye are the realities], especially the [essence] of the Beautiful and Good.

Just as the eye cannot see God, so can it not behold the Beautiful and Good. For that they are integral parts of God, wedded to Him alone, inseparate familiars, most beloved, with whom God is Himself in love, or they with God.

5. If thou canst God conceive, thou shalt conceive the Beautiful and Good, transcending Light, made lighter than the Light by God. That Beauty is beyond compare, imitate that Good, e'en as God is Himself.

As, then, thou dost conceive of God, conceive the Beautiful and Good. For they cannot be joined with aught of other things that live, since they can never be divorced from God.

Seek'st thou for God, thou seekest for the Beautiful. One is the Path that leadeth unto It—Devotion joined with Gnosis.

6. And thus it is that they who do not know and do not tread Devotion's Path, do dare to call man beautiful and good, though he have ne'er e'en in his visions seen a whit that's Good, but is enveloped with every kind of bad, and thinks the bad is good, and thus doth make unceasing use of it, and even feareth that it should be ta'en from him, so straining every nerve not only to preserve but even to increase it.

Such are the things that men call good and beautiful,

Asclepius—things which we cannot flee or hate; for hardest thing of all is that we've need of them and cannot live without them.

VII. The Greatest Ill Among Men Is Ignorance of God

1. Whither stumble ye, sots, who have sopped up the wine of ignorance and can so far not carry it that ye already even spew it forth?

    Stay ye, be sober, gaze upwards with the [true] eyes of the heart! And if ye cannot all, yet ye at least who can!

    For that the ill of ignorance doth pour o'er all the earth and overwhelm the soul that's battened down within the body, preventing it from fetching port within Salvation's harbors.

2. Be ye then not carried off by the fierce flood, but using the shore-current ye who can, make for Salvation's port, and, harboring there, seek ye for one to take you by the hand and lead you unto Gnosis' gates.

    Where shines clear Light, of every darkness clean; where not a single soul is drunk, but sober all they gaze with their hearts' eyes on Him who willeth to be seen.

    No ear can hear Him, nor can eye see Him, nor tongue speak of Him, but [only] mind and heart.

    But first thou must tear off from thee the cloak which thou dost wear—the web of ignorance, the ground of bad, corruption's chain, the carapace of darkness, the living death, sensation's corpse, the tomb thou carriest with thee, the robber in thy house, who through the things he loveth, hateth thee, and through the things he hateth, bears thee malice.

3. Such is the hateful cloak thou wearest—that throttles thee [and holds thee] down to it, in order that thou may'st not gaze above, and having seen the Beauty of the Truth, and Good that dwells therein, detest the bad of it; having found out the plot that it hath schemed against thee, by making void of sense those seeming things which men think senses.

For that it hath with mass of matter blocked them up and crammed them full of loathsome lust, so that thou may'st not hear about the things that thou should'st hear, nor see the things thou should'st see.

VIII. That No One of Existing Things doth Perish, but Men in Error Speak of Their Changes as Destructions and as Deaths

1. [Hermes:] Concerning Soul and Body, son, we now must speak; in what way Soul is deathless, and whence comes the activity in composing and dissolving Body.

For there's no death for aught of things [that are]; the thought this word conveys, is either void of fact, or [simply] by the knocking off a syllable what is called "death", doth stand for "deathless".

For death is of destruction, and nothing in the Cosmos is destroyed. For if Cosmos is second God, a life that cannot die, it cannot be that any part of this immortal life should die. All things in Cosmos are parts of Cosmos, and most of all is man, the rational animal.

2. For truly first of all, eternal and transcending birth, is God the universals' Maker. Second is he "after His image", Cosmos, brought into being by Him, sustained and fed by Him,

made deathless, as by his own Sire, living for aye, as ever free from death.

Now that which ever-liveth, differs from the Eternal; for He hath not been brought to being by another, and even if He have been brought to being, He hath not been brought to being by Himself, but ever is brought into being.

For the Eternal, in that It is eternal, is the all. The Father is Himself eternal of Himself, but Cosmos hath become eternal and immortal by the Father.

3. And of the matter stored beneath it, the Father made of it a universal body, and packing it together made it spherical—wrapping it round the life—[a sphere] which is immortal in itself, and that doth make materiality eternal.

But He, the Father, full-filled with His ideas, did sow the lives into the sphere, and shut them in as in a cave, willing to order forth the life with every kind of living.

So He with deathlessness enclosed the universal body, that matter might not wish to separate itself from body's composition, and so dissolve into its own [original] unorder.

For matter, son, when it was yet incorporate, was in unorder. And it doth still retain down here this [nature of unorder] enveloping the rest of the small lives—that increase-and-decrease which men call death.

4. It is round earthly lives that this unorder doth exist. For that the bodies of the heavenly ones preserve one order allotted to them by the Father as their rule; and it is by the restoration of each one [of them] this order is preserved indissolute.

The "restoration" of bodies on the earth is thus their composition, whereas their dissolution restores them to those bodies which can never be dissolved, that is to say, which know no death. Privation, thus, of sense is brought about, not loss of bodies.

5.   Now the third life—Man, after the image of the Cosmos made, [and] having mind, after the Father's will, beyond all earthly lives—not only doth have feeling with the second God, but also hath conception of the first; for of the one 'tis sensible as of a body, while of the other it conceives as bodiless and the Good Mind.

Tat: Doth then this life not perish?

Hermes: Hush, son! and understand what God, what Cosmos [is], what is a life that cannot die, and what a life subject to dissolution.

Yea, understand the Cosmos is by God and in God; but Man by Cosmos and in Cosmos.

The source and limit and the constitution of all things is God.

IX. On Thought and Sense

1.   I gave the Perfect Sermon (Logos) yesterday, Asclepius; today I think it right, as sequel thereunto, to go through point by point the Sermon about Sense.

Now sense and thought do seem to differ, in that the former has to do with matter, the latter has to do with substance. But unto me both seem to be at-one and not to differ—in men I mean. In other lives sense is at-oned with Nature, but in men thought.

Now mind doth differ just as much from thought as God doth from divinity. For that divinity by God doth come to be, and by mind thought, the sister of the word (logos) and instruments of one another. For neither doth the word (logos) find utterance without thought, nor is thought manifested without word.

2. So sense and thought both flow together into man, as though they were entwined with one another. For neither without sensing can one think, nor without thinking sense.

But it is possible [they say] to think a thing apart from sense, as those who fancy sights in dreams. But unto me it seems that both of these activities occur in dream-sight, and sense doth pass out of the sleeping to the waking state.

For man is separated into soul and body, and only when the two sides of his sense agree together, does utterance of its thought conceived by mind take place.

3. For it is mind that doth conceive all thoughts—good thoughts when it receives the seeds from God, their contraries when [it receiveth them] from the daimonials; no part of Cosmos being free of daimon, who stealthily doth creep into the daimon who's illumined by God's light, and sow in him the seed of its own energy.

And mind conceives the seed thus sown, adultery, murder, parricide, [and] sacrilege, impiety, [and] strangling, casting down precipices, and all such other deeds as are the work of evil daimons.

4. The seeds of God, 'tis true, are few, but vast and fair, and good—virtue and self-control, devotion. Devotion is God-gnosis; and he who knoweth God, being filled with all good things, thinks godly thoughts and not thoughts like the many [think].

For this cause they who Gnostic are, please not the many, nor the many them. They are thought mad and laughted at; they're hated and despised, and sometimes even put to death.

For we did say that bad must needs dwell on earth, where 'tis in its own place. Its place is earth, and not Cosmos, as some will sometimes say with impious tongue.

But he who is a devotee of God, will bear with all—once he has sensed the Gnosis. For such an one all things, e'en though they be for others bad, are for him good; deliberately he doth refer them all unto the Gnosis. And, thing most marvelous, 'tis he alone who maketh bad things good.

5. But I return once more to the Discourse (Logos) on Sense. That sense doth share with thought in man, doth constitute him man. But 'tis not [every] man, as I have said, who benefits by thought; for this man is material, that other one substantial.

For the material man, as I have said, [consorting] with the bad, doth have his seed of thought from daimons; while the substantial men [consorting] with the Good, are saved by God.

Now God is Maker of all things, and in His making, He maketh all [at last] like to Himself; but they, while they're becoming good by exercise of their activity, are unproductive things.

It is the working of the Cosmic Course that maketh their becomings what they are, befouling some of them with bad and others of them making clean with good.

For Cosmos, too, Asclepius, possesseth sense-and-thought peculiar to itself, not like that of man; 'tis not so manifold, but as it were a better and a simpler one.

6. The single sense-and-thought of Cosmos is to make all things, and make them back into itself again, as Organ of the Will of God, so organized that it, receiving all the seeds into itself from God, and keeping them within itself, may make

all manifest, and [then] dissolving them, make them all new again; and thus, like a Good Gardener of Life, things that have been dissolved, it taketh to itself, and giveth them renewal once again.

There is no thing to which it gives not life; but taking all unto itself it makes them live, and is at the same time the Place of Life and its Creator.

7. Now bodies matter [-made] are in diversity. Some are of earth, of water some, some are of air, and some of fire.

But they are all composed; some are more [composite], and some are simpler. The heavier ones are more [composed], the lighter less so.

It is the speed of Cosmos' Course that works the manifoldness of the kinds of births. For being a most swift Breath, it doth bestow their qualities on bodies together with the One Pleroma—that of Life.

8. God, then, is Sire of Cosmos; Cosmos, of all in Cosmos. And Cosmos is God's Son; but things in Cosmos are by Cosmos.

And properly hath it been called Cosmos [Order]; for that it orders all with their diversity of birth, with its not leaving aught without its life, with the unweariedness of its activity, the speed of its necessity, the composition of its elements, and order of its creatures.

The same, then, of necessity and propriety should have the name of Order.

The sense-and-thought, then, of all lives doth come into them from without, inbreathed by what contains [them all]; whereas Cosmos receives them once for all together with its coming into being, and keeps them as a gift from God.

9. But God is not, as some suppose, beyond the reach of sense-

and-thought. It is through superstition men thus impiously speak.

For all the things that are, Asclepius, all are in God, are brought by God to be, and do depend on Him—both things that act through bodies, and things that through soul-substance make [other things] to move, and things that make things live by means of spirit, and things that take unto themselves the things that are worn out.

And rightly so; nay, I would rather say, He doth not have these things; but I speak forth the truth, He is them all Himself. He doth not get them from without, but gives them out [from Him].

This is God's sense-and-thought, ever to move all things. And never time shall be when e'en a whit of things that are shall cease; and when I say "a whit of things that are", I mean a whit of God. For things that are, God hath; nor aught [is there] without Him, nor [is] He without aught.

10. These things should seem to thee, Asclepius, if thou dost understand them, true; but if thou dost not understand, things not to be believed.

To understand is to believe, to not believe is not to understand.

My word (logos) doth go before [thee] to the truth. But mighty is the mind, and when it hath been led by word up to a certain point, it hath the power to come before [thee] to the truth.

And having thought o'er all these things, and found them consonant with those which have already been translated by the reason, it hath [e'en now] believed, and found its rest in that Fair Faith.

To those, then, who by God['s good aid] do understand the things that have been said [by us] above, they're credible; but unto those who understand them not, incredible.

Let so much, then, suffice on thought-and-sense.

X. The Key

1. Hermes: My yesterday's discourse (logos) I did devote to thee, Asclepius, and so 'tis [only] right I should devote today's to Tat; and this the more because 'tis the abridgement of the General Sermons (Logoi) which he has had addressed to him.

"God, Father and the Good", then, Tat, hath the same nature, or more exactly, energy.

For nature is a predicate of growth, and used of things that change, both mobile and immobile, that is to say, both human and divine, each one of which He willeth into being.

But energy consists in something else, as we have shown in treating of the rest, both things divine and human things; which thing we ought to have in mind when treating of the Good.

2. God's energy is then His Will; further His essence is to will the being of all things. For what is "God and Father and the Good" but the "to be" of all that are not yet? Nay, subsistence self of everything that is; this, then, is God, this Father, this the Good; to Him is added naught of all the rest.

And though the Cosmos, that is to say the Sun, is also sire himself to them that share in him; yet so far is he not the cause of good unto the lives, he is not even of their living.

So that e'en if he be a sire, he is entirely so by compulsion of the Good's Good-will, apart from which nor being nor becoming could e'er be.

3. Again, the parent is the children's cause, both on the father's and the mother's side, only by sharing in the Good's desire [that doth pour] through the Sun. It is the Good which doeth the creating.

And such a power can be possessed by no one else than Him alone who taketh naught, but wills all things to be; I will not, Tat, say "makes".

For that the maker is defective for long periods (in which he sometimes makes, and sometimes doth not make) both in the quality and in the quantity [of what he makes]; in that he sometimes maketh them so many and such like, and sometimes the reverse.

But "God and Father and the Good" is [cause] for all to be. So are at least these things for those who can see.

4. For It doth will to be, and It is both Itself and most of all by reason of Itself. Indeed, all other things beside are just bacause of It; for the distinctive feature of the Good is "that it should be known". Such is the Good, O Tat.

Tat: Thou hast, O father, filled us so full of this so good and fairest sight, that thereby my mind's eye hath now become for me almost a thing to worship.

For that the vision of the Good doth not, like the sun's beam, firelike blaze on the eyes and make them close; nay, on the contrary, it shineth forth and maketh to increase the seeing of the eye, as far as e'er a man hath the capacity to hold the inflow of the radiance that the mind alone can see.

Not only does it come more swiftly down to us, but it does us no harm, and is instinct with all immortal life.

5.   They who are able to drink in a somewhat more than others of this Sight, ofttimes from out the body fall asleep in this fairest Spectacle, as was the case with Uranus and Cronus, our forebears. May this be our lot too, O father mine!

Hermes: Yea, may it be, my son! But as it is, we are not yet strung to the Vision, and not as yet have we the power in our mind's eye to unfold and gaze upon the Beauty of the Good—Beauty that naught can e'er corrupt or any comprehend.

For only then wilt thou upon It gaze when thou canst say no word concerning It. For Gnosis of the Good is holy silence and a giving holiday to every sense.

6.   For neither can he who perceiveth It, perceive aught else; nor he who gazeth on It, gaze on aught else; nor hear aught else, nor stir his body any way. Staying his body's every sense and every motion he stayeth still.

And shining then all round his mond, It shines through his whole soul, and draws it out of body, transforming all of him to essence.

For it is possible, my son, that a man's soul should be made like to God, e'en while it still is in a body, if it doth contemplate the Beauty of the Good.

7.   Tat: Made like to God? What dost thou, father, mean?

Hermes: Of every soul apart are transformations, son.

Tat: What meanest thou? Apart?

Hermes: Didst thou not, in the General Sermons, hear that from one Soul—the All-soul—come all these souls which are made to revolve in all the cosmos, as though divided off?

Of these souls, then, it is that there are many changes, some to a happier lot and some to [just] the contrary of this.

Thus some that were creeping things change into things that in the water dwell, the souls of water things change to earth-dwellers, those that live on earth change to things with wings, and souls that live in air change to men, while human souls reach the first step of deathlessness changed into daimones.

And so they circle to the choir of the Inerrant Gods; for of the Gods there are two choirs, the one Inerrant, and the other Errant. And this is the most perfect glory of the soul.

8. But if a soul on entering the body of a man persisteth in its vice, it neither tasteth deathlessness nor shareth in the Good; but speeding back again it turns into the path that leads to creeping things. This is the sentence of the vicious soul.

And the soul's vice is ignorance. For that the soul who hath no knowledge of the things that are, or knowledge of their nature, or of Good, is blinded by the body's passions and tossed about.

This wretched soul, not knowing what she is, becomes the slave of bodies of strange form in sorry plight, bearing the body as a load; not as the ruler, but the ruled. This [ignorance] is the soul's vice.

9. But on the other hand the virtue of the soul is Gnosis. For he who knows, he good and pious is, and still while on the earth divine.

Tat: But who is such an one, O father mine?

Hermes: He who doth not say much or lend his ear to much. For he who spendeth time in arguing and hearing arguments, doth shadow-fight. For "God, the Father and the Good", is not to be obtained by speech or hearing.

And yet though this is so, there are in all the beings senses, in that they cannot without senses be.

But Gnosis is far different from sense. For sense is brought about by that which hath the mastery o'er us, while Gnosis is the end of science, and science is God's gift.

10. All science is incorporeal, the instrument it uses being the mind, just as the mind employs the body.

Both then come into bodies, [I mean] both things that are cognizable by mind alone and things material. For all things must consist out of antithesis and contrariety; and this can otherwise not be.

Tat: Who then is this material God of whom thou speakest?

Hermes: Cosmos is beautiful, but is not good—for that it is material and freely passible; and though it is the first of all things passible, yet is it in the second rank of being and wanting in itself.

And though it never hath itself its birth in time, but ever is, yet is its being in becoming, becoming for all time the genesis of qualities and quantities; for it is mobile and all material motion's genesis.

11. It is intelligible rest that moves material motion in this way, since Cosmos is a sphere—that is to say, a head. And naught of head above's material, as naught of feet below's intelligible, but all material.

And head itself is moved in a sphere-like way—that is to say, as head should move, is mind.

All then that are united to the "tissue" of this "head" (in

which is soul) are in their nature free from death—just as when body hath been made in soul, are things that hath more soul than body.

Whereas those things which are at greater distance from this "tissue"—there, where are things which have a greater share of body than of soul—are by their nature subject unto death.

The whole, however, is a life; so that the universe consists of both the hylic and of the intelligible.

12. Again, the Cosmos is the first of living things, while man is second after it, though first of things subject to death.

Man hath the same ensouling power in him as all the rest of living things; yet is he not only not good, but even evil, for that he's subject unto death.

For though the Cosmos also is not good in that it suffers motion, it is not evil, in that it is not subject to death. But man, in that he's subject both to motion and to death, is evil.

13. Now then the principles of man are this-wise vehicled: mind in the reason (logos), the reason in the soul, soul in the spirit, and spirit in the body.

Spirit pervading [body] by means of veins and arteries and blood, bestows upon the living creature motion, and as it were doth bear it in a way.

For this cause some do think the soul is blood, in that they do mistake its nature, not knowing that [at death] it is this spirit that must first withdraw into the soul, whereon the blood congeals and veins and arteries are emptied, and then the living creature is withdrawn; and this is the body's death.

14. Now from one Source all things depend; while Source [dependeth] from the One and Only [One]. Source is, moreover,

moved to become Source again; whereas the One standeth perpetually and is not moved.

Three then are they: "God, the Father and the Good", Cosmos and man.

God doth contain Cosmos; Cosmos [containeth] man. Cosmos is e'er God's Son, man as it were Cosmos' child.

15. Not that, however, God ignoreth man; nay, right well doth He know him, and willeth to be known.

This is the sole salvation for a man—God's Gnosis. This is the Way Up to the Mount.

By Him alone the soul becometh good, not whiles is good, whiles evil, but [good] out of necessity.

Tat: What dost thou mean, Thrice-greatest one?

Hermes: Behold an infant's soul, my son, that is not yet cut off, because its body is still small and not as yet come unto its full bulk.

Tat: How?

Hermes: A thing of beauty altogether is [such a soul] to see, not yet befouled by body's passions, still all but hanging from the Cosmic Soul!

But when the body grows in bulk and draweth down the soul into its mass, then doth the soul cut off itself and bring upon itself forgetfulness, and no more shareth in the Beautiful and the Good. And this forgetfulness becometh vice.

16. It is the same for them who go out from the body.

For when the soul withdraws into itself, the spirit doth contract itself within the blood, and the soul within the spirit. And then the mind, stripped of its wrappings, and naturally divine, taking unto itself a fiery body, doth traverse every space, after abandoning the soul unto its judgement and whatever chastisement it hath deserved.

Tat: What dost thou, father, mean by this? The mind is parted from soul and soul from spirit? Whereas thou said'st the soul was the mind's vesture, and the soul's the spirit.

17. Hermes: The hearer, son, should think with him who speaks and breathe with him; nay, he should have a hearing subtler than the voice of him who speaks.

It is, son, in a body made of earth that this arrangement of the vestures comes to pass. For in a body made of earth it is impossible the mind should take its seat itself by its own self in nakedness.

For neither is it possible on the one hand the earthly body should contain so much immortality, nor on the other that so great a virtue should endure a body passible in such close contact with it. It taketh, then, the soul for as it were an envelope.

And soul itself, being too and thing divine, doth use the spirit as its envelope, while spirit doth pervade the living creature.

18. When then the mind doth free itself from the earth-body, it straightway putteth on its proper robe of fire, with which it could not dwell in an earth-body.

For earth doth not bear fire; for it is all set in a blaze even by a small spark. And for this cause is water poured around earth, to be a guard and wall, to keep the blazing of the fire away.

But mind, the swiftest thing of all divine outthinkings, and swifter than all elements, hath for its body fire.

For mind being builder doth use the fire as tool for the construction of all things—the Mind of all [for the construction] of all things, but that of man only for things on earth.

Stript of its fire the mind on earth cannot make things divine, for it is human in its dispensation.

19. The soul in man, however—not every soul, but one that pious is—is a daimonic something and divine.

And such a soul when from the body freed, if it have fought the fight of piety—the fight of piety is to know God and to do wrong to no man—such a soul becomes entirely mind.

Whereas the impious soul remains in its own essence, chastised by its own self, and seeking for an earthly body where to enter, if only it be human.

For that no other body can contain a human soul; nor is it right that any human soul should fall into the body of a thing that doth possess no reason. For that the law of God is this: to guard the human soul from such tremendous outrage.

20. Tat: How father, then, is a man's soul chastised?

Hermes: What greater chastisement of any human soul can there be, son, than lack of piety? What fire has so fierce a flame as lack of piety? What ravenous beast so mauls the body as lack of piety the very soul?

Dost thou not see what hosts of ills the impious soul doth bear?

It shrieks and screams: I burn; I am ablaze; I know not what to cry or do; ah, wretched me, I am devoured by all the ills that compass me about; alack, poor me, I neither see nor hear!

Such are the cries wrung from a soul chastised; not, as the many think, and thou, son, dost suppose, that a [man's] soul, passing from body, is changed into a beast.

Such is a very grave mistake, for that the way a soul doth suffer chastisement is this:

21. When mind becomes a daimon, the law requires that it should take a fiery body to execute the services of God; and entering in the soul most impious it scourgeth it with whips made of its sins.

And then the impious soul, scourged with its sins, is plunged in murders, outrage, blasphemy, in violence of all kinds, and all the other things whereby mankind is wronged.

But on the pious soul the mind doth mount and guide it to the Gnosis' Light. And such a soul doth never tire in songs of praise [to God] and pouring blessing on all men, and doing good in word and deed to all, in imitation of its Sire.

22. Wherefore, my son, thou shouldst give praise to God and pray that thou mayst have thy mind Good Mind. It is, then, to a better state the soul doth pass; it cannot to a worse.

Further there is an intercourse of souls; those of the gods have intercourse with those of men, and those of men with souls of creatures which possess no reason.

The higher, further, have in charge the lower; the gods look after men, men after animals irrational, while God hath charge of all; for He is higher than them all and all are less than He.

Cosmos is subject, then, to God, man to the Cosmos, and irrationals to man. But God is o'er them all, and God contains them all.

God's rays, to use a figure, are His energies; the Cosmos's are natures, the arts and sciences are man's.

The energies act through the Cosmos, thence through the nature-rays of Cosmos upon man; the nature-rays [act] through the elements, man [acteth] through the sciences and arts.

23. This is the dispensation of the universe, depending from the nature of the One, pervading [all things] through the Mind, than which is naught diviner nor of greater energy; and naught a greater means for the at-oning men to gods and gods to men.

He, [Mind,] is the Good Daimon. Blessed the soul that is most filled with Him, and wretched is the soul that's empty of the Mind.

Tat: Father, what dost thou mean, again?

Hermes: Dost think then, son, that every soul hath the Good [Mind]? For 'tis of Him we speak, not of the mind in service of which we were just speaking, the mind sent down for [the soul's] chastisement.

24. For soul without the mind "can neither speak nor act". For oftentimes the mind doth leave the soul, and at that time the soul neither sees nor understands, but is just like a thing that hath no reason. Such is the power of mind.

Yet doth it not endure a sluggish soul, but leaveth such a soul tied to the body and bound tight down by it. Such soul, my son, doth not have Mind; and therefore such an one should not be called a man. For that man is a thing-of-life divine; man is not measured with the rest of lives of things upon the earth, but with the lives above in heaven, who are called gods.

Nay more, if we must boldly speak the truth, the true

"man" is e'en higher than the gods, or at the [very] least the gods and men are very whit in power each with the other equal.

25. For no one of the gods in heaven shall come down to the earth, o'er-stepping heaven's limit; whereas man doth mount up to heaven and measure it; he knows what things of it are high, what things are low, and learns precisely all things else besides. And greater thing than all; without e'en quitting earth, he doth ascend above. So vast a sweep doth he possess of ecstasy.

For this cause can a man dare say that man on earth is god subject to death, while god in heaven is man from death immune.

Wherefore the dispensation of all things is brought about by means of there, the twain—Cosmos and Man—but by the One.

XI. Mind Unto Hermes

1. Mind: Master this sermon (logos), then, Thrice-greatest Hermes, and bear in mind the spoken words; and as it hath come unto Me to speak, I will no more delay.

Hermes: As many men say many things, and these diverse, about the All and Good, I have not learned the truth. Make it, then, clear to me, O Master mine! For I can trust the explanation of these things, which comes from Thee alone.

2. Mind: Hear [then], My son, how standeth God and All.

God; Aeon; Cosmos; Time; Becoming.

God maketh Aeon; Aeon, Cosmos; Cosmos, Time; and Time, Becoming.

The Good—the Beautiful, Wisdom, Blessedness—is essence, as it were, of God; of Aeon, Sameness; of Cosmos, Order; of Time, Change; and of Becoming, Life and Death.

The energies of God are Mind and Soul; of Aeon, lastingness and deathlessness; of Cosmos, restoration and the opposite thereof; of Time, increase and decrease; and of Becoming, quality.

Aeon is, then, in God; Cosmos, in Aeon; in Cosmos; Time; in Time, Becoming.

Aeon stands firm round God; Cosmos is moved in Aeon; Time hath its limits in the Cosmos; Becoming doth become in Time.

3. The source, therfore, of all is God; their essence, Aeon; their matter, Cosmos.

God's power is Aeon; Aeon's work is Cosmos—which never hath become, yet ever doth become by Aeon.

Therefore will Cosmos never be destroyed, for Aeon's indestructible; nor doth a whit of things in Cosmos perish, for Cosmos is enwrapped by Aeon round on every side.

Hermes: But God's Wisdom—what is that?

Mind: The Good and Beautiful, and Blessedness, and Virtue's all, and Aeon.

Aeon, then, ordereth [Cosmos], imparting deathlessness and lastingness to matter.

4. For its beginning doth depend on Aeon, as Aeon doth on God.

Now Genesis and Time, in Heaven and upon the Earth, are of two natures.

In Heaven they are unchangeable and indestructible, but on the Earth they're subject unto change and to destruction.

Further, the Aeon's soul is God; the Cosmos' soul is Aeon; the Earth's soul, Heaven.

And God in Mind; and Mind, in Soul; and Soul, in Matter; and all of them through Aeon.

But all this Body, in which are all the bodies, is full of Soul; and Soul is full of Mind, and Mind of God.

It fills it from within, and from without encircles it, making the All to live.

Without, this vast and perfect Life [encircles] Cosmos; within, it fills [it with] all lives; above, in Heaven, continuing in sameness; below, on Earth, changing becoming.

5. And Aeon doth preserve this [Cosmos], or by Necessity, or by Foreknowledge, or by Nature, or by whatever else a man supposes or shall suppose. And all is this—God energizing.

The Energy of God is Power that naught can e'er surpass, a Power with which no one can make comparison of any human thing at all, or any thing divine.

Wherefore, O Hermes, never think that aught of things above or things below is like to God, for thou wilt fall from truth. For naught is like to That which hath no like, and is Alone and One.

And do not ever think that any other can possibly possess His power; for what apart from Him is there of life, and deathlessness and change of quality? For what else should He make?

God's not inactive, since all things [then] would lack activity; for all are full of God.

But neither in the Cosmos anywhere, nor in aught else, is there inaction. For that "inaction" is a name that cannot be applied to either what doth make or what is made.

6. But all things must be made; both ever made, and also in accordance with the influence of every space.

For He who makes, is in them all; not stablished in some one of them, nor making one thing only, but making all.

For being Power, He energizeth in the things He makes and is not independent of them—although the things He makes are subject to Him.

Now gaze through Me upon the Cosmos that's now subject to thy sight; regard its Beauty carefully—Body in pure perfection, though one than which there's no more ancient one, ever in prime of life, and ever-young, nay, rather, in even fuller and yet fuller prime!

7. Behold, again, the seven subject Worlds; ordered by Aeon's order, and with their varied course full-filling Aeon!

[See how] all things [are] full of light, and nowhere [is there] fire; for 'tis the love and the blending of the contraries and the dissimilars that doth give birth to light down shining by the energy of God, the Father of all good, the Leader of all order, and Ruler of the seven world-orderings!

[Behold] the Moon, forerunner of them all, the instrument of nature, and the transmuter of its lower matter!

[Look at] the Earth set in the midst of All, foundation of the Cosmos Beautiful, feeder and nurse of things on Earth!

And contemplate the multitude of deathless lives, how great it is, and that of lives subject to death; and midway, between both, immortal [lives] and mortal, [see thou] the circling Moon.

8. And all are full of soul, and all are moved by it, each in its proper way; some round the Heaven, others around the Earth;

[see] how the right [move] not unto the left, nor yet the left unto the right; nor the above below, nor the below above.

And that all there are subject unto Genesis, My dearest Hermes, thou hast no longer need to learn of Me. For that they bodies are, have souls, and they are moved.

But 'tis impossible for them to come together into one without some one to bring them [all] together. It must, then, be that such a one as this must be some one who's wholly One.

9. For as the many motions of them [all] are different, and as their bodies are not like, yet has one speed been ordered for them all, it is impossible that there should be two or more makers for them.

For that one single order is not kept among "the many"; but rivalry will follow of the weaker with the stronger, and they will strive.

And if the maker of the lives that suffer change and death, should be another, he would desire to make the deathless ones as well; just as the maker of the deathless ones, [to make the lives] that suffer death.

But come! if there be two—if matter's one, and Soul is one, in whose hands would there be the distribution for the making? Again, if both of them have some of it, in whose hands may be the greater part?

10. But thus conceive it, then; that every living body doth consist of soul and matter, whether [that body be] of an immortal, or a mortal, or an irrational [life].

For that all living bodies are ensouled; whereas, upon the other hand, those that live not, are matter by itself.

And, in like fashion, Soul when in its self is, after its own maker, cause of life; but the cause of all life is He who makes the things that cannot die.

Hermes: How, then, is it that, first, lives subject to death are other than the deathless ones? And, next, how is it that Life which knows no death, and maketh deathlessness, doth not make animals immortal?

11. Mind: First, that there is some one who does these things, is clear; and, next, that He is also One, is very manifest. For, also, Soul is one, and Life is one, and Matter one.

Hermes: But who is He?

Mind: Who may it other be than the One God? Whom else should it beseem to put Soul into lives but God alone? One, then, is God.

It would indeed be most ridiculous, if when thou dost confess the Cosmos to be one, Sun one, Moon one, and Godhead one, thou shouldst wish God Himself to be some one or other of a number!

12. All things, therefore, He makes, in many [ways]. And what great thing is it for God to make life, soul, and deathlessness, and change, when thou [thyself] dost do so many things?

For thou dost see, and speak, and hear, and smell, and taste, and touch, and walk, and think, and breathe. And it is not one man who smells, another one who walks, another one who thinks, and [yet] another one who breathes. But one is he who doth all these.

And yet no one of these could be apart from God. For just as, should thou cease from these, thou wouldst no longer be a living thing, so also, should God cease from them (a thing not law to say), no longer is He God.

13. For if it hath been shown that no thing can [inactive] be, how much less God? For if there's aught he doth not make (if it be law to say), He is imperfect. But if He is not only not inactive, but perfect [God], then He doth make all things.

Give thou thyself to Me, My Hermes, for a little while, and thou shalt understand more easily how that God's work is one, in order that all things may be—that are being made, or once have been, or that are going to be made. And this is, My beloved, Life; this is the Beautiful; this is the Good; this, God.

14. And if thou wouldst in practice understand [this work], behold what taketh place with thee desiring to beget. Yet this is not like unto that, for He doth not enjoy.

For that indeed He hath no other one to share in what He works, for working by Himself, He ever is at work, Himself being what He doth. For did He separate Himself from it, all things would [then] collapse, and all must die, Life ceasing.

But if all things are lives, and also Life is one; then, one is God. And, furthermore, if all are lives, both those in Heaven and those on Earth, and One Life in them all is made to be by God, and God is it—then, all are made by God.

Life is the making-one of Mind and Soul; accordingly Death is not the destruction of those that are at-oned, but the dissolving of their union.

15. Aeon, moreover, is God's image; Cosmos [is] Aeon's; the Sun, of Cosmos; and Man, [the image] of the Sun.

The people call change death, because the body is dissolved, and life, when it's dissolved, withdraws to the unmanifest. But in this sermon (logos), Hermes, My beloved, as thou dost hear, I say the Cosmos also suffers change—for that a part of it each day is made to be in the unmanifest—yet it is ne'er dissolved.

These are the passions of the Cosmos—revolvings and concealments; revolving is conversion and concealment renovation.

16. The Cosmos is all-formed—not having forms external to itself, but changing them itself within itself. Since, then, Cosmos is made to be all-formed, what may its maker be? For that, on the one hand, He should not be void of all form; and, on the other hand, if He's all-formed, He will be like the Cosmos. Whereas, again, has He a single form, He will thereby be less than Cosmos.

What, then, say we He is?—that we may not bring round our sermon (logos) into doubt; for naught that mind conceives of God is doubtful.

He, then, hath one idea, which is His own alone, which doth not fall beneath the sight, being bodiless, and [yet] by means of bodies manifesteth all [ideas]. And marvel not that there's a bodiless idea.

17. For it is like the form of reason (logos) and mountain-tops in pictures. For they appear to stand out strongly from the rest, but really are quite smooth and flat.

And now consider what is said more boldly, but more truly!

Just as man cannot live apart from Life, so neither can God live without [His] doing good. For this is as it were the life and motion as it were of God—to move all things and make them live.

18. Now some of the things said should bear a sense peculiar to

themselves. So understand, for instance, what I'm going to say.

All are in God, [but] not as lying in a place. For place is both a body and immovable, and things that lie do not have motion.

Now things lie one way in the bodiless, another way in being made manifest.

Think, [then,] of Him who doth contain them all; and think, that than the bodiless naught is more comprehensive, or swifter, or more potent, but it is the most comprehensive, the swiftest, and most potent of them all.

19. And, thus, think from thyself, and bid thy soul go unto any land, and there more quickly than thy bidding will it be. And bid it journey oceanwards; and there, again, immediately 'twill be, not as if passing on from place to place, but as if being there.

And bid it also mount to heaven; and it will need no wings, not will aught hinder it, nor fire of sun, nor auther, nor vortex-swirl, nor bodies of the other stars; but, cutting through them all, it will soar up to the last Body [of them all]. And shouldst thou will to break through this as well, and contemplate what is beyond—if there be aught beyond the Cosmos; it is permitted thee.

20. Behold what power, what swiftness, thou dost have! And canst thou do all of these things, and God not [do them]?

Then, in this way know God; as having all things in Himself as thoughts, the whole Cosmos itself.

If, then, thou dost not make thyself like unto God, thou canst not know Him. For like is knowable unto like [alone].

Make, [then,] thyself to grow to the same stature as the Greatness which transcends all measure; leap forth from every body; transcend all time; become Eternity; and [thus] shalt thou know God.

Conceiving nothing is impossible unto thyself, think thyself deathless and able to know all—all arts, all sciences, the way of every life.

Become more lofty than all height, and lower than all depth. Collect into thyself all senses of [all] creatures—of fire, [and] water, dry and moist. Think that thou art at the same time in every place—in earth, in sea, in sky; not yet begotten, in the womb, young, old, [and] dead, in after-death conditions.

And if thou knowest all these things at once—times, places, doings, qualities, and quantities; thou canst know God.

21. But if thou lockest up thy soul within thy body, and dost debase it, saying: I nothing know; I nothing can; I fear the sea; I cannot scale the sky; I know not who I was, who I shall be—what is there [then] between [thy] God and thee?

For thou canst know naught of things beautiful and good so long as thou dost love thy body and art bad.

The greatest bad there is, is not to know God's Good; but to be able to know [Good], and will, and hope, is a Straight Way, the Good's own [Path], both leading there and easy.

If thou but settest thy foot thereon, 'twill meet thee everywhere, 'twill everywhere be seen, both where and when thou dost expect it not—waking, sleeping, sailing, journeying, by night, by day, speaking, [and] saying naught. For there is naught that is not the image of the Good.

22. Hermes: Is God unseen?

Mind: Hush! Who is more manifest than He? For this one

reason hath He made all things, that through them all thou mayest see Him.

This is the Good of God, this [is] His Virtue—that He may be manifest through all.

For naught's unseen, even of things that are without a body. Mind sees itself in thinking, God in making.

So far these things have been made manifest to thee, Thrice-greatest one! Reflect on all the rest in the same way with thyself, and thou shalt not be led astray.

XII. About The Common Mind

1. Hermes: The Mind, O Tat, is of God's very essence—(if such a thing as essence of God there be)—and what that is, it and it only knows precisely.

   The Mind, then, is not separated off from God's essentiality, but is united to it, as light to sun.

   This Mind in men is God, and for this cause some of mankind are gods, and their humanity is nigh unto divinity.

   For the Good Daimon said: "Gods are immortal men, and men are mortal gods."

2. But in irrational lives Mind is their nature. For where is Soul, there too is Mind; just as where Life, there is there also Soul.

   But in irrational lives their soul is life devoid of mind; for Mind is the in-worker of the souls of men for good—He works on them for their own good.

   In lives irrational He doth co-operate with each one's nature; but in the souls of men He counteracteth them.

   For every soul, when it becomes embodied, is instantly depraved by pleasure and by pain.

For in a compound body, just like juices, pain and pleasure seethe, and into them the soul, on entering in, is plunged.

3. O'er whatsoever souls the Mind doth, then, preside, to these it showeth its own light, by acting counter to their prepossessions, just as a good physician doth upon the body prepossessed by sickness, pain inflict, burning or lancing it for sake of health.

In just the selfsame way the Mind inflicteth pain on the soul, to rescue it from pleasure, whence comes its every ill.

The great ill of the soul is godlessness; then followeth fancy for all evil things and nothing good.

So, then, Mind counteracting it doth work good on the soul, as the physician health upon the body.

4. But whatsoever human souls have not the Mind as pilot, they share in the same fate as souls of lives irrational.

For [Mind] becomes co-worker with them, giving full play to the desires toward which [such souls] are borne—[desires] that from the rush of lust strain after the irrational; [so that such human souls,] just like irrational animals, cease not irrationally to rage and lust, nor are they ever satiate of ills.

For passions and irrational desires are ills exceeding great; and over these God hath set up the Mind to play the part of judge and executioner.

5. Tat: In that case, father mine, the teaching (logos) as to Fate, which previously thou didst explain to me, risks to be overset.

For that if it be absolutely fated for a man to fornicate, or commit sacrilege, or do some other evil deed, why is he punished—when he hath done the deed from Fate's necessity?

Hermes: All works, my son, are Fate's; and without Fate naught of things corporal—or good, or ill—can come to pass.

But it is fated, too, that he who doeth ill, shall suffer. And for this cause he doth it—that he may suffer what he suffereth, because he did it.

6. But for the moment, [Tat,] let be the teaching as to vice and Fate, for we have spoken of these things in other [of our sermons]; but now our teaching (logos) is about the Mind:— what Mind can do, and how it is [so] different—in men being such and such, and in irrational lives [so] changed; and [then] again that in irrational lives it is not of a beneficial nature, while that in men it quencheth out the wrathful and the lustful elements. Of men, again, we must class some as led by reason, and others as unreasoning.

7. But all men are subject to Fate, and genesis and change, for these are the beginning and the end of Fate.

And though all men do suffer fated things, those led by reason (those whom we said Mind doth guide) do not endure like suffering with the rest; but, since they've freed themselves from viciousness, not being bad, they do not suffer bad.

Tat: How meanest thou again, my father? Is not the fornicator bad; the murderer bad; and [so with] all the rest?

Hermes: [I meant not that;] but that the Mind-led man, my son, though not a fornicator, will suffer just as though he had committed fornication, and though he be no murderer, as though he had committed murder.

The quality of change he can no more escape than that of genesis.

But it is possible for one who hath the Mind, to free himself from vice.

8. Wherefore I've ever heard, my son, Good Daimon also say—
    (and had He set it down in written words, He would have
    greatly helped the race of men; for He alone, my son, doth
    truly, as the Firstborn God, gazing on all things, give voice to
    words (logoi) divine)—yea, once I heard Him say:

    "All things are one, and most of all the bodies which the
    mind alone perceives. Our life is owing to [God's] Energy
    and Power and Aeon. His Mind is good, so is His Soul as
    well.

    And this being so, intelligible things know naught of sep-
    aration. So, then, Mind, being Ruler of all things, and being
    Soul of God, can do whate'er it wills."

9. So do thou understand, and carry back this word (logos) unto
    the question thou didst ask before—I mean about Mind's
    Fate.

    For if thou dost with accuracy, son, eliminate [all] cap-
    tious arguments (logoi), thou wilt discover that of every truth
    the Mind, the Soul of God, doth rule o'er all—o'er Fate, and
    Law, and all things else; and nothing is impossible to it—
    neither o'er Fate to set a human soul, nor under Fate to set [a
    soul] neglectful of what comes to pass. Let this so far suffice
    from the Good Daimon's most good [words].

    Tat: Yea, [words] divinely spoken, father mine, truly and
    helpfully. But further still explain me this.

10. Thou said'st that Mind in lives irrational worked in them as
    [their] nature, co-working with their impulses.

    But impulses of lives irrational, as I do think, are passions.

    Now if the Mind co-worketh with [these] impulses, and
    if the impulses of [lives] irrational be passions, then is Mind
    also passion, taking its color from the passions.

Hermes: Well put, my son! Thou questionest right nobly, and it is just that I as well should answer [nobly].

11. All things incorporeal when in a body are subject unto passion, and in the proper sense they are [themselves] all passions.

For every thing that moves itself is incorporeal; while every thing that's moved is body.

Incorporeals are further moved by Mind, and movement's passion.

Both, then, are subject unto passion—both mover and the moved, the former being ruler and the latter ruled.

But when a man hath freed himself from body, then is he also freed from passion.

But, more precisely, son, naught is impassible, but all are passible.

Yet passion differeth from passibility; for that the one is active, while the other's passive. Incorporeals moreover act upon themselves, for either they are motionless or they are moved; but whichsoe'er it be, it's passion.

But bodies are invariably acted on, and therefore they are passible.

Do not, then, let terms trouble thee; action and passion are both the selfsame thing. To use the fairer sounding term, however, does no harm.

12. Tat: Most clearly hast thou, father mine, set forth the teaching (logos).

Hermes: Consider this as well, my son; that these two things God hath bestowed on man beyond all mortal lives—both mind and speech (logos) equal to immortality. He hath the mind for knowing God and uttered speech (logos) for eulogy of Him.

And if one useth these for what he ought, he'll differ not a whit from the immortals. Nay, rather, on departing from the body, he will be guided by the twain unto the Choir of Gods and Blessed Ones.

13. Tat: Why, father mine!—do not the other lives make use of speech (logos)?

Hermes: Nay, son; but use of voice; speech is far different from voice. For speech is general among all men, while voice doth differ in each class of living thing.

Tat: But with men also, father mine, according to each race, speech differs.

Hermes: Yea, son, but man is one; so also speech is one and is interpreted, and it is found the same in Egypt, and in Persia, and in Greece.

Thou seemest, son, to be in ignorance of Reason's (Logos) worth and greatness. For that the Blessed God, Good Daimon, hath declared:

"Soul is in Body, Mind in Soul; but Reason (Logos) is in Mind, and Mind in God; and God is Father of [all] these."

14. The Reason, then, is the Mind's image, and Mind God's [image]; while Body is [the image] of the Form; and Form [the image] of the Soul.

The subtlest part of Matter is, then, Air; of Air, Soul; of Soul, Mind; and of Mind, God. And God surroundeth all and permeateth all; while Mind Surroundeth Soul, Soul Air, Air Matter.

Necessity and Providence and Nature are instruments of Cosmos and of Matter's ordering; while of intelligible things each is Essence, and Sameness is their Essence. But of the bodies of the Cosmos each is many; for through possessiong

Sameness, [these] composed bodies, though they do change from one into another of themselves, do natheless keep the incorruption of their Sameness.

15. Whereas in all the rest of composed bodies, of each there is a certain number; for without number structure cannot be, or composition, or decomposition.

Now it is units that give birth to number and increase it, and, being decomposed, are taken back again into themselves.

Matter is one; and this whole Cosmos—the mighty God and image of the mightier One, both with Him unified, and the conserver of the Will and Order of the Father—is filled full of Life.

Naught is there in it throughout the whole of Aeon, the Father's [everlasting].

Re-establishment—nor of the whole, nor of the parts—which doth not live.

For not a single thing that's dead, hath been, or is, or shall be in [this] Cosmos.

For that the Father willed it should have Life as long as it should be. Wherefore it needs must be a God.

16. How then, O son, could there be in the God, the image of the Father, in the plenitude of Life—dead things?

For that death is corruption, and corruption destruction.

How then could any part of that which knoweth no corruption be corrupted, or any whit of him the God destroyed?

Tat: Do they not, then, my father, die—the lives in it, that are its parts?

Hermes: Hush, son!—led into error by the term in use for what takes place.

They do not die, my son, but are dissolved as compound bodies.

Now dissolution is not death, but dissolution of a compound; it is dissolved not so that it may be destroyed, but that it may become renewed.

For what is the activity of life? Is it not motion? What then in Cosmos is there that hath no motion? Naught is there, son!

17. Tat: Doth not Earth even, father, seem to thee to have no motion?

Hermes: Nay, son; but rather that she is the only thing which, though in very rapid motion, is also stable.

For how would it not be a thing to laugh at, that the Nurse of all should have no motion, when she engenders and brings forth all things?

For 'tis impossible that without motion one who doth engender, should do so.

That thou should ask if the fourth part is not inert, is most ridiculous; for the body which doth have no motion, gives sign of nothing but inertia.

18. Know, therefore, generally, my son, that all that is in Cosmos is being moved for increase or for decrease.

Now that which is kept moving, also lives; but there is no necessity that that which lives, should be all same.

For being simultaneous, the Cosmos, as a whole, is not subject to change, my son, but all its parts are subject unto it; yet naught [of it] is subject to corruption, or destroyed.

It is the terms employed that confuse men. For 'tis not genesis that constituteth life, but 'tis sensation; it is not change that constituteth death, but 'tis forgetfulness.

Since, then, these things are so, they are immortal all—
Matter, [and] Life, [and] Spirit, Mind [and] Soul, of which
whatever liveth, is composed.

19. Whatever then doth live, oweth its immortality unto the
Mind, and most of all doth man, he who is both recipient of
God, and co-essential with Him.

For with this life alone doth God consort; by visions in
the night, by tokens in the day, and by all things doth He
foretell the future unto him—by birds, by inward parts, by
wind, by tree.

Wherefore doth man lay claim to know things past, things
present and to come.

20. Observe this too, my son; that each one of the other lives
inhabiteth one portion of the Cosmos—aquatic creatures
water, terrene earth, and aery creatures air; while man doth
use all these—earth, water air [and] fire; he seeth Heaven, too,
and doth contact it with [his] sense.

But God surroundeth all, and permeateth all, for He is
energy and power; and it is nothing difficult, my son, to conceive God.

21. But if thou wouldst Him also contemplate, behold the ordering of the Cosmos, and [see] the orderly behavior of its
ordering; behold thou the Necessity of things made manifest, and [see] the Providence of things become and things
becoming; behold how Matter is all-full of Life; [behold]
this so great God in movement, with all the good and noble
[ones]—gods, daimones and men!

Tat: But these are purely energies, O father mine!

Hermes: If, then, they're purely energies, my son—by
whom, then, are they energized except by God?

THE BOOK OF HERMETICA

Or art thou ignorant, that just as Heaven, Earth, Water, Air, are parts of Cosmos, in just the selfsame way God's parts are Life and Immortality, [and] Energy, and Spirit, and Necessity, and Providence, and Nature, Soul, and Mind, and the Duration of all these that is called Good?

And there are naught of things that have become, or are becoming, in which God is not.

22. Tat: Is He in Matter, father, then?

Hermes: Matter, my son, is separate from God, in order that thou may'st attribute to it the quality of space. But what thing else than mass think'st thou it is, if it's not energized?

Whereas if it be energized, by whom is it made so? For energies, we said, are parts of God.

By whom are, then, all lives enlivened? By whom are things immortal made immortal?

By whom changed things made changeable?

And whether thou dost speak of Matter, of Body, or of Essence, know that these too are energies of God; and that materiality is Matter's energy, that corporeality is Bodies' energy, and that essentiality doth constituteth the energy of Essence; and this is God—the All.

23. And in the All is naught that is not God. Wherefore nor size, nor space, nor quality, nor form, nor time, surroundeth God; for He is All, and All surroundeth all, and permeateth all.

Unto this Reason (Logos), son, thy adoration and thy worship pay. There is one way alone to worship God; [it is] not to be bad.

XIII. The Secret Sermon on the Mountain

1. Tat: [Now] in the General Sermons, father, thou didst speak in riddles most unclear, conversing on Divinity; and when thou saidst no man could e'er be saved before Rebirth, thy meaning thou didst hide.

    Further, when I became thy Suppliant, in Wending up the Mount, after thou hadst conversed with me, and when I longed to learn the Sermon (Logos) on Rebirth (for this beyond all other things is just the thing I know not), thou saidst, that thou wouldst give it me—"when thou shalt have become a stranger to the world".

    Wherefore I got me ready and made the thought in me a stranger to the world-illusion.

    And now do thou fill up the things that fall short in me with what thou saidst would give me the tradition of Rebirth, setting it forth in speech or in the secret way.

    I know not, O Thrice-greatest one, from out what matter and what womb Man comes to birth, or of what seed.

2. Hermes: Wisdom that understands in silence [such is the matter and the womb from out which Man is born], and the True Good the seed.

    Tat: Who is the sower, father? For I am altogether at a loss.

    Hermes: It is the Will of God, my son.

    Tat: And of what kind is he that is begotten, father? For I have no share of that essence in me, which doth transcend the senses. The one that is begot will be another one from God, God's Son?

    Hermes: All in all, out of all powers composed.

Tat: Thou tellest me a riddle, father, and dost not speak as father unto son.

Hermes: This Race, my son, is never taught; but when He willeth it, its memory is restored by God.

3. Tat: Thou sayest things impossible, O father, things that are forced. Hence answers would I have direct unto these things. Am I a son strange to my father's race?

Keep it not, father, back from me. I am a true-born son; explain to me the manner of Rebirth.

Hermes: What may I say, my son? I can but tell thee this. Whene'er I see within myself the Simple Vision brought to birth out of God's mercy, I have passed through myself into a Body that can never die. And now I am not as I was before; but I am born in Mind.

The way to do this is not taught, and it cannot be seen by the compounded element by means of which thou seest.

Yea, I have had my former composed form dismembered for me. I am no longer touched, but I have touch; I have dimension too; and [yet] am I a stranger to them now.

Thou seest me with eyes, my son; but what I am thou dost not understand [even] with fullest strain of body and of sight.

4. Tat: Into fierce frenzy and mind-fury hast thou plunged me, father, for now no longer do I see myself.

Hermes: I would, my son, that thou hadst e'en passed right through thyself, as they who dream in sleep yet sleepless.

Tat: Tell me this too! Who is the author of Rebirth?

Hermes: The Son of God, the One Man, by God's Will.

5. Tat: Now hast thou brought me, father, unto pure stupe-

faction. Arrested from the senses which I had before, ... for [now] I see thy Greatness identical with thy distinctive form.

Hermes: Even in this thou art untrue; the mortal form doth change with every day. 'Tis turned by time to growth and waning, as being an untrue thing.

6. Tat: What then is true, Thrice-greatest One?

Hermes: That which is never troubled, son, which cannot be defined; that which no color hath, nor any figure, which is not turned, which hath no garment, which giveth light; that which is comprehensible unto itself [alone], which doth not suffer change; that which no body can contain.

Tat: In very truth I lose my reason, father. Just when I thought to be made wise by thee, I find the senses of this mind of mine blocked up.

Hermes: Thus is it, son: That which is upward borne like fire, yet is borne down like earth, that which is moist like water, yet blows like air, how shalt thou this perceive with sense—the that which is not solid nor yet moist, which naught can bind or loose, of which in power and energy alone can man have any notion—and even then it wants a man who can perceive the Way of Birth in God?

7. Tat: I am incapable of this, O father, then?

Hermes: Nay, God forbid, my son! Withdraw into thyself, and it will come; will, and it comes to pass; throw out of work the body's senses, and thy Divinity shall come to birth; purge from thyself the brutish torments—things of matter.

Tat: I have tormentors then in me, O father?

Hermes: Ay, no few, my son; nay, fearful ones and manifold.

Tat: I do not know them, father.

Hermes: Torment the first is this Not-knowing, son; the second one is Grief; the third, Intemperance; the fourth, Concupiscence; the fifth, Unrighteousness; the sixth is Avarice; the seventh, Error; the eighth is Envy; the ninth, Guile; the tenth is Anger; eleventh, Rashness; the twelfth is Malice.

These are in number twelve; but under them are many more, my son; and creeping through the prison of the body they force the man that's placed therein to suffer in his senses. But they depart (though not all at once) from him who hath been taken pity on by God; and this it is which constitutes the manner of Rebirth. And . . . the Reason (Logos).

8. And now, my son, be still and solemn silence keep! Thus shall the mercy that flows on us from God not cease.

Henceforth rejoice, O son, for by the Powers of God thou art being purified for the articulation of the Reason (Logos).

Gnosis of God hath come to us, and when this comes, my son, Not-knowing is cast out.

Gnosis of Joy hath come to us, and on its coming, son, Sorrow will flee away to them who give it room. The Power that follows Joy do I invoke, thy Self-control. O Power most sweet! Let us most gladly bid it welcome, son! How with its coming doth it chase Intemperance away!

9. Now fourth, on Continence I call, the Power against Desire. This step, my son, is Righteousness' firm seat. For without judgement see how she hath chased Unrighteousness away. We are made righteous, son, by the departure of Unrighteousness.

Power sixth I call to us—that against Avarice, Sharing-with-all.

And now that Avarice is gone, I call on Truth. And Error flees, and Truth is with us.

See how [the measure of] the Good is full, my son, upon Truth's coming. For Envy is gone from us; and unto Truth is joined the Good as well, with Life and Light.

And now no more doth any torment of the Darkness venture nigh, but vanquished [all] have fled with whirring wings.

10. Thou knowest [now], my son, the manner of Rebirth. And when the Ten is come, my son, that driveth out the Twelve, the Birth in understanding is complete, and by this birth we are made into Gods.

Who then doth by His mercy gain this Birth in God, abandoning the body's senses, knows himself [to be of Light and Life] and that he doth consist of these, and [thus] is filled with bliss.

11. Tat: By God made steadfast, father, no longer with the sight my eyes afford I look on things, but with the energy the Mind doth give me through the Powers.

In Heaven am I, in earth, in water, air; I am in animals, in plants; I'm in the womb, before the womb, after the womb; I'm everywhere!

But further tell me this: How are the torments of the Darkness, when they are twelve in number, driven out by the ten Powers? What is the way of it, Thrice-greatest one?

12. Hermes: This dwelling-place through which we have just passed, my son, is constituted from the circle of the twelve types-of-life, this being composed of elements, twelve in number, but of one nature, an omniform idea. For man's delusion there are disunions in them, son, while in their action

they are one. Not only can we never part Rashness from Wrath; they cannot even be distinguished.

According to right reason (logos), then, they naturally withdraw once and for all, in as much as they are chased out by no less than ten powers, that is, the Ten.

For, son, the Ten is that which giveth birth to souls. And Life and Light are unified there, where the One hath being from the Spirit. According then to reason (logos) the One contains the Ten, the Ten the One.

13. Tat: Father, I see the All, I see myself in Mind.

Hermes: This is, my son, Rebirth—no more to look on things from body's view-point (a thing three ways in space extended) ... though this Sermon (Logos) on Rebirth, on which I did not comment—in order that we may not be calumniators of the All unto the multitude, to whom indeed God Himself doth will we should not.

14. Tat: Tell me, O father: This Body which is made up of the Powers, is it at any time dissolved?

Hermes: Hush, [son]! Speak not of things impossible, else wilt thou sin and thy Mind's eye be quenched.

The natural body which our sense perceives is far removed from this essential birth.

The first must be dissolved, the last can never be; the first must die, the last death cannot touch.

Dost thou not know thou hast been born a God, Son of the One, even as I myself?

15. Tat: I would, O father, hear the Praise-giving with hymn which thou didst say thou heardest then when thou wert at the Eight [the Ogdoad] of Powers

Hermes: Just as the Shepherd did foretell [I should], my son, [when I came to] the Eight.

Well dost thou haste to "strike thy tent", for thou hast been made pure.

The Shepherd, Mind of all masterhood, hath not passed on to me more than hath been written down, for full well did he know that I should of myself be able to learn all, and hear what I should wish, and see all things.

He left to me the making of fair things; wherefore the Powers within me, e'en as they are in all, break into song.

16. Tat: Father, I wish to hear; I long to know these things.

Hermes: Be still, my son; hear the Praise-giving now that keeps [the soul] in tune, Hymn of Re-birth—a hymn I would not have thought fit so readily to tell, had'st thou not reached the end of all.

Wherefore this is not taught, but is kept hid in silence.

Thus then, my son, stand in a place uncovered to the sky, facing the southern wind, about the sinking of the setting sun, and make thy worship; so in like manner too when he doth rise, with face to the east wind.

Now, son, be still!

The Secret Hymnody

17. Let every nature of the World receive the utterance of my hymn!

Open thou Earth! Let every bolt of the Abyss be drawn for me. Stir not, ye Trees!

I am about to hymn creation's Lord, both All and One.

Ye Heavens open and ye Winds stay still; [and] let God's deathless Sphere receive my word (logos)!

For I will sing the praise of Him who founded all; who fixed the Earth, and hung up Heaven, and gave command that Ocean should afford sweet water [to the Earth], to both those parts that are inhabited and those that are not, for the support and use of every man; who made the Fire to shine for gods and men for every act.

Let us together all give praise to Him, sublime above the Heavens, of every nature Lord!

'Tis He who is the Eye of Mind; may He accept the praise of these my Powers!

18. Ye powers that are within me, hymn the One and All; sing with my Will, Powers all that are within me!

O blessed Gnosis, by thee illumined, hymning through thee the Light that mond alone can see, I joy in Joy of Mind.

Sing with me praises all ye Powers!

Sing praise, my Self-control; sing thou through me, my Righteousness, the praises of the Righteous; sing thou, my Sharing-all, the praises of the All; through me sing, Truth, Truth's praises!

Sing thou, O Good, the Good! O Life and Light, from us to you our praises flow!

Father, I give Thee thanks, to Thee Thou Energy of all my Powers; I give Thee thanks, O God, Thou Power of all my Energies!

19. Thy Reason (Logos) sings through me Thy praises. Take back through me the All into [Thy] Reason—[my] reasonable oblation!

Thus cry the Powers in me. They sing Thy praise, Thou All; they do Thy Will.

From Thee Thy Will; to Thee the All. Receive from all

their reasonable oblation. The All that is in us, O Life, pre-serve; O Light, illumine it; O God, in-spirit it.

It is Thy Mind that plays the shepherd to Thy Word, O Thou Creator, Bestower of the Spirit [upon all].

20. [For] Thou art God, Thy Man thus cries to Thee through Fire, through Air, through Earth, through Water, [and] through Spirit, through Thy creatures.

'Tis from Thy Aeon I have found praise-giving; and in thy Will, the object of my search, have I found rest.

Tat: By thy good pleasure have I seen this praise-giving being sung, O father; I have set it in my Cosmos too.

Hermes: Say in the Cosmos that thy mind alone can see, my son.

Tat: Yea, father, in the Cosmos that the mind alone can see; for I have been made able by thy Hymn, and by thy Praise-giving my mind hath been illumined. But further I myself as well would from my natural mind send praise-giving to God.

21. Hermes: But not unheedfully, my son.

Tat: Aye. What I behold in mind, that do I say.

To thee, thou Parent of my Bringing into Birth, as unto God I, Tat, send reasonable offerings. O God and Father, thou art the Lord, thou art the Mind. Receive from me oblations reasonable as thou would'st wish; for by thy Will all things have been perfected.

Hermes: Send thou oblation, son, acceptable to God, the Sire of all; but add, my son, too, "through the Word" (Logos).

Tat: I give thee, father, thanks for showing me to sing such hymns.

22. Hermes: Happy am I, my son, that though hast brought the good fruits forth of Truth, products that cannot die. And now

that thou hast learnt this lesson from me, make promise to keep silence on thy virtue, and to no soul, my son, make known the handing on to thee the manner of Rebirth, that we may not be thought to be calumniators.

And now we both of us have given heed sufficiently, both I the speaker and the hearer thou.

In Mind hast thou become a Knower of thyself and our [common] Sire.

THE EMERALD TABLET

Multiple Translations

Contents

CONTENTS

HISTORY OF THE TABLET

History of the Tablet (largely summarised from Needham 1980, Holmyard 1957).

The Tablet probably first appeared in the West in editions of the psuedo-Aristotelian Secretum Secretorum which was actually a translation of the Kitab Sirr al-Asar, a book of advice to kings which was translated into latin by Johannes Hispalensis c. 1140 and by Philip of Tripoli c. 1243.

Other translations of the Tablet may have been made during the same period by Plato of Tivoli and Hugh of Santalla, perhaps from different sources.

The date of the Kitab Sirr al-Asar is uncertain, though c. 800 has been suggested and it is not clear when the tablet became part of this work.

Holmyard was the first to find another early arabic version (Ruska found a 12th centruy recension claiming to have been dictated by Sergius of Nablus) in the Kitab Ustuqus al-Uss al-Thani (Second Book of the Elements of Foundation) attributed to Jabir. Shortly after Ruska found another version appended to the Kitab Sirr al-Khaliqa wa San'at al-Tabi'a (Book of the Secret of Creation and the Art of Nature), which is also known as the Kitab Balaniyus al-Hakim fi'l-'Ilal (book of Balinas the wise on the Causes). It has been proposed that this book may have been written as early as 650, and was definitely finished by the Caliphate of al-Ma'mun (813–33).

Scholars have seen similarities between this book and the Syriac Book of Treasures written by Job of Odessa (9th century) and more interestingly the Greek writings of the bishop Nemesius of Emesa in Syria from the mid fourth century. However though this suggests a possible Syriac source, none of these writings contain the tablet.

Balinas is usually identified with Apollonius of Tyna, but there is little evidence to connect him with the Kitab Balabiyus, and even if there was, the story implies that Balinas found the tablet rather than wrote it, and the recent discoveries of the dead sea scrolls and the nag hamamdi texts suggest that hiding texts in caves is not impossible, even if we did not have the pyramids before us.

Ruska has suggested an origin further east, and Needham has proposed an origin in China.

Holmyard, Davis and Anon all consider that this Tablet may be one of the earliest of all alchemical works we have that survives.

It should be remarked that apparently the Greeks and Egyptians used the termtranslated as 'emerald' for emeralds, green granites, "and perhaps green jasper". In medieval times the emerald table of the Gothic kings of Spain, and the Sacro catino–a dish said to have belonged to the Queen of Sheba, to have been used at the last supper, and to be made of emerald, were made of green glass [Steele and Singer: 488].

Translations From Jabir ibn Hayyan.

0. Balinas mentions the engraving on the table in the hand of Hermes, which says:

1. Truth! Certainty! That in which there is no doubt!

2. That which is above is from that which is below, and that which is below is from that which is above, working the miracles of one.

3. As all things were from one.

4. Its father is the Sun and its mother the Moon.

5. The Earth carried it in her belly, and the Wind nourished it in her belly, 7) as Earth which shall become Fire.

7a. Feed the Earth from that which is subtle, with the greatest power.

8. It ascends from the earth to the heaven and becomes ruler over that which is above and that which is below.

14. And I have already explained the meaning of the whole of this in two of these books of mine.

[Holmyard 1923: 562.]

Another Arabic Version (from the German of Ruska, translated by 'Anonymous').

0. Here is that which the priest Sagijus of Nabulus has dictated concerning the entrance of Balinas into the hidden chamber ... After my entrance into the chamber, where the talisman was set up, I came up to an old man sitting on a golden throne, who was holding an emerald tablet in one hand.

   And behold the following—in Syriac, the primordial language-was written thereon:

1. Here (is) a true explanation, concerning which there can be no doubt.

2. It attests: The above from the below, and the below from the above—the work of the miracle of the One.

3. And things have been from this primal substance through a single act. How wonderful is this work! It is the main (principle) of the world and is its maintainer.

4. Its father is the sun and its mother the moon; the

5. wind has borne it in its body, and the earth has nourished it.

6. the father of talismen and the protector of miracles

6a. whose powers are perfect, and whose lights are confirmed (?),

7. a fire that becomes earth.

7a. Separate the earth from the fire, so you will attain the subtle as more inherent than the gross, with care and sagacity.

8. It rises from earth to heaven, so as to draw the lights of the heights to itself, and descends to the earth; thus within it are the forces of the above and the below;

9. because the light of lights within it, thus does the darkness flee before it.

10. The force of forces, which overcomes every subtle thing and penetrates into everything gross.

11. The structure of the microcosm is in accordance with the structure of the macrocosm.

12. And accordingly proceed the knowledgeable.

13. And to this aspired Hermes, who was threefold graced with wisdom.

14. And this is his last book, which he concealed in the chamber.

[Anon 1985: 24–5]

Twelfth Century Latin

0. When I entered into the cave, I received the tablet zaradi, which was inscribed, from between the hands of Hermes, in which I discovered these words:

1. True, without falsehood, certain, most certain.

2. What is above is like what is below, and what is below is like that which is above. To make the miracle of the one thing.

3. And as all things were made from contemplation of one, so all things were born from one adaptation.

4. Its father is the Sun, its mother is the Moon.

5. The wind carried it in its womb, the earth breast fed it.

6. It is the father of all 'works of wonder' (Telesmi) in the world.

6a. Its power is complete (integra).

7. If cast to (turned towards–versa fuerit) earth,

7a. it will separate earth from fire, the subtile from the gross.

8. With great capacity it ascends from earth to heaven. Again it descends to earth, and takes back the power of the above and the below.

9. Thus you will receive the glory of the distinctiveness of the world. All obscurity will flee from you.

10. This is the whole most strong strength of all strength, for it overcomes all subtle things, and penetrates all solid things.

11a. Thus was the world created.

12. From this comes marvelous adaptions of which this is the proceedure.

13. Therefore I am called Hermes, because I have three parts of the wisdom of the whole world.

14. And complete is what I had to say about the work of the Sun, from the book of Galieni Alfachimi.

[From Latin in Steele and Singer 1928: 492.]

Translation from Aurelium Occultae Philosophorum. Georgio Beato

1. This is true and remote from all cover of falsehood
2. Whatever is below is similar to that which is above. Through this the marvels of the work of one thing are procured and perfected.
3. Also, as all things are made from one, by the condsideration of one, so all things were made from this one, by conjunction.
4. The father of it is the sun, the mother the moon.
5. The wind bore it in the womb. Its nurse is the earth, the mother of all perfection.
6a. Its power is perfected.
7. If it is turned into earth,
7a. separate the earth from the fire, the subtle and thin from the crude and course, prudently, with modesty and wisdom.
8. This ascends from the earth into the sky and again descends from the sky to the earth, and receives the power and efficacy of things above and of things below.
9. By this means you will acquire the glory of the whole world, and so you will drive away all shadows and blindness.
10. For this by its fortitude snatches the palm from all other fortitude and power. For it is able to penetrate and subdue everything subtle and everything crude and hard.
11a. By this means the world was founded

12. and hence the marvelous cojunctions of it and admirable effects, since this is the way by which these marvels may be brought about.

13. And because of this they have called me Hermes Tristmegistus since I have the three parts of the wisdom and Philsosphy of the whole universe.

14. My speech is finished which I have spoken concerning the solar work [Davis 1926: 874.]

Translation of Issac Newton c. 1680.

1. Tis true without lying, certain most true.

2. That wch is below is like that wch is above that wch is above is like yt wch is below to do ye miracles of one only thing.

3. And as all things have been arose from one by ye mediation of one: so all things have their birth from this one thing by adaptation.

4. The Sun is its father, the moon its mother,

5. the wind hath carried it in its belly, the earth its nourse.

6. The father of all perfection in ye whole world is here.

7. Its force or power is entire if it be converted into earth.

7a. Seperate thou ye earth from ye fire, ye subtile from the gross sweetly wth great indoustry.

8. It ascends from ye earth to ye heaven again it desends to ye earth and receives ye force of things superior inferior.

9. By this means you shall have ye glory of ye whole world thereby all obscurity shall fly from you.

10. Its force is above all force. For it vanquishes every subtle thing penetrates every solid thing.

11a. So was ye world created.

12. From this do come admirable adaptaions whereof ye means (Or process) is here in this.

13. Hence I am called Hermes Trismegist, having the three parts of ye philosophy of ye whole world.

14. That wch I have said of ye operation of ye Sun is accomplished ended.

[Dobbs 1988: 183–4.]

Translation from Kriegsmann (?) alledgedly from the Phoenician

1. I speak truly, not falsely, certainly and most truly

2. These things below with those above and those with these join forces again so that they produce a single thing the most wonderful of all.

3. And as the whole universe was brought forth from one by the word of one GOD, so also all things are regenerated perpetually from this one according to the disposition of Nature.

4. It has the Sun for father and the Moon for mother:

5. it is carried by the air as if in a womb, it is nursed by the earth.

6. It is the cause, this, of all perfection of all things throughout the universe.

6a. This will attain the highest perfection of powers

7. if it shall be reduced into earth

7a. Distribute here the earth and there the fire, thin out the density of this the suavest (suavissima) thing of all.

8. Ascend with the greatest sagacity of genius from the earth into the sky, and thence descend again to the earth, and rec-

ognise that the forces of things above and of things below are one,

9. so as to posses the glory of the whole world-and beyond this man of abject fate may have nothing further.

10. This thing itself presently comes forth stronger by reasons of this fortitude: it subdues all bodies surely, whether tenuous or solid, by penetrating them.

11a. And so everything whatsoever that the world contains was created.

12. Hence admirable works are accomplished which are instituted (carried out-instituuntur) according to the same mode.

13. To me therefor the name of Hermes Trismegistus has been awarded because I am discovered as the Teacher of the three parts of the wisdom of the world.

14. These then are the considerations which I have concluded ought to be written down concerning the readiest operations of the Chymic art.

[Davis 1926: 875 slightly modified.]

From Sigismund Bacstrom (allegedly translated from Chaldean).

0. The Secret Works of CHIRAM ONE in essence, but three in aspect.

1. It is true, no lie, certain and to be depended upon,

2. the superior agrees with the inferior, and the inferior agrees with the superior, to effect that one truly wonderful work.

3. As all things owe their existence to the will of the only one, so all things owe their origin to the one only thing, the most hidden by the arrangement of the only God.

4. The father of that one only thing is the sun its mother is the moon,

5. the wind carries it in its belly; but its nourse is a spirituous earth.

6. That one only thing is the father of all things in the Universe.

6a. Its power is perfect,

7. after it has been united with a spirituous earth.

7a. Separate that spirituous earth from the dense or crude by means of a gentle heat, with much attention.

8. In great measure it ascends from the earth up to heaven, and descends again, newborn, on the earth, and the superior and the inferior are increased in power.

9. By this wilt thou partake of the honours of the whole world. And Darkness will fly from thee.

10. This is the strength of all powers. With this thou wilt be able to overcome all things and transmute all what is fine and what is coarse.

11a. In this manner the world was created;

12. the arrangements to follow this road are hidden.

13. For this reason I am called Chiram Telat Mechasot, one in essence, but three in aspect. In this trinity is hidden the wisdom of the whole world.

14. It is ended now, what I have said concerning the effects of the sun. Finish of the Tabula Smaragdina.

[See Hall 1977: CLVIII,]

From Madame Blavatsky

2. What is below is like that which is above, and what is above is similar to that which is below to accomplish the wonders of the one thing.

3. As all things were produced by the mediation of one being, so all things were produced from this one by adaption.

4. Its father is the sun, its mother the moon.

6a. It is the cause of all perfection throughout the whole earth.

7. Its power is perfect if it is changed into earth.

7a. Separate the earth from the fire, the subtile from the gross, acting prudently and with judgement.

8. Ascend with the greatest sagacity from earth to heaven, and unite together the power of things inferior and superior;

9. thus you will possess the light of the whole world, and all obscurity will fly away from you.

10. This thing has more fortitude than fortitude itself, because it will overcome every subtile thing and penetrate every solid thing.

11a. By it the world was formed.

[Blavatsky 1972: 507.]

From Fulcanelli (translated from the French by Sieveking)

1. This is the truth, the whole truth and nothing but the truth:-

2. As below, so above; and as above so below. With this knowledge alone you may work miracles.

3. And since all things exist in and eminate from the ONE Who is the ultimate Cause, so all things are born after their kind from this ONE.

4. The Sun is the father, the Moon the mother;

5. the wind carried it in his belly. Earth is its nurse and its guardian.

6. It is the Father of all things,

6a. the eternal Will is contained in it.

7. Here, on earth, its strength, its power remain one and undivided.

7a. Earth must be separated from fire, the subtle from the dense, gently with unremitting care.

8. It arises from the earth and descends from heaven; it gathers to itself the strength of things above and things below.

9. By means of this one thing all the glory of the world shall be yours and all obscurity flee from you.

10. It is power, strong with the strength of all power, for it will penetrate all mysteries and dispel all ignorance.

11a. By it the world was created.

12. From it are born manifold wonders, the means to achieving which are here given

13. It is for this reason that I am called Hermes Trismegistus; for I possess the three essentials of the philosophy of the universe.

14. This is is the sum total of the work of the Sun.

[Sadoul 1972: 25–6.]

From Fulcanelli, new translation

1. It is true without untruth, certain and most true:
2. that which is below is like that which is on high, and that which is on high is like that which is below; by these things are made the miracles of one thing.
3. And as all things are, and come from One, by the mediation of One, So all things are born from this unique thing by adaption.
4. The Sun is the father and the Moon the mother.
5. The wind carries it in its stomach. The earth is its nourisher and its receptacle.
6. The Father of all the Theleme of the universal world is here.
6a. Its force, or power, remains entire,
7. if it is converted into earth.
7a. You separate the earth from the fire, the subtle from the gross, gently with great industry.
8. It climbs from the earth and descends from the sky, and receives the force of things superior and things inferior.
9. You will have by this way, the glory of the world and all obscurity will flee from you.
10. It is the power strong with all power, for it will defeat every subtle thing and penetrate every solid thing
11a. In this way the world was created.
12. From it are born wonderful adaptations, of which the way here is given.
13. That is why I have been called Hermes Tristmegistus, having the three parts of the universal philosophy.
14. This, that I have called the solar Work, is complete.

[Translated from Fulcanelli 1964: 312.]

From Idres Shah

1. The truth, certainty, truest, without untruth.

2. What is above is like what is below. What is below is like what is above. The miracle of unity is to be attained.

3. Everything is formed from the contemplation of unity, and all things come about from unity, by means of adaptation.

4. Its parents are the Sun and Moon.

5. It was borne by the wind and nurtured by the Earth.

6. Every wonder is from it

6a. and its power is complete.

7. Throw it upon earth,

7a. and earth will separate from fire. The impalpable separated from the palpable.

8. Through wisdom it rises slowly from the world to heaven. Then it descends to the world combining the power of the upper and the lower.

9. Thus you will have the illumination of all the world, and darkness will disappear.

10. This is the power of all strength-it overcomes that which is delicate and penetrates through solids.

11a. This was the means of the creation of the world.

12. And in the future wonderful developements will be made, and this is the way.

13. I am Hermes the Threefold Sage, so named because I hold the three elements of all wisdom.

14. And thus ends the revelation of the work of the Sun.

(Shah 1964: 198).

Hypothetical Chinese Original

1. True, true, with no room for doubt, certain, worthy of all trust.

2. See, the highest comes from the lowest, and the lowest from the highest; indeed a marvelous work of the tao.

3. See how all things originated from It by a single process.

4. The father of it (the elixir) is the sun (Yang), its mother the moon (Yin).

5. The wind bore it in its belly, and the earth nourished it.

6. This is the father of wondrous works (changes and transformations), the guardian of mysteries,

6a. perfect in its powers, the animator of lights.

7. This fire will be poured upon the earth . . .

7a. So separate the earth from the fire, the subtle from the gross, acting prudently and with art.

8. It ascends from the earth to the heavens (and orders the lights above), then descends again to the earth; and in it is the power of the highest and the lowest.

9. Thus when you have the light of lights darkness will flee away from you.

10. With this power of powers (the elixir) you shall be able to get the mastery of every subtle thing, and be able to penetrate everything that is gross.

11a. In this way was the great world itself formed.

12. Hence thus and thus marvellous operations will be acheived.

[Slightly altered from Needham 1980: 371.]

TEXTUAL REMARKS

On #3 Some Latin texts have meditatione (contemplation), others mediatione (mediation). Some texts have adaptatione (by adaptation), some have adoptionis (by adoption).

On #6 'Telesmi' is a greek word, some texts have 'thelesmi'.

On #6, 7 In some texts 'Its Power is Complete' is a separate line. In the generally accepted reading, this runs into #7 producing 'Its Power is complete if versa fuerit to earth'. Where possible this has been indicated by dividing these lines in 6, 6a, 7, 7a On #7, 8 In some texts the 'Wisdom, capacity' (magno ingenio) is read as referring to #7, and hence the operation of Separation is to be carried out 'carefully', in other readings the 'wisdom' is held to refer to #8 and the product of the Separation which thus ascends with 'wisdom'.

Needham quotes Ruska to the effect that sections 3, 12 and 14 are probably late additions (op. cit)

COMMENTARIES

On #1 Hortulanus: ". . . the most true Sun is procreated by art. And he says most true in the superlative degree because the Sun generated by this art exceeds all natural Sun in all of its properties, medicinal and otherwise" (Davis modified by 'Linden')

On #2 Albertus Magnus: Hermes says "the powers of all things below originate in the stars and constellations of the heavens: and that all these powers are poured down into all things below by the circle called Alaur, which is, they said, the first circle of the constellations". This descent is "noble when the materials receiving these powers are more like things above in their brightness and transparency; ignoble when the materials are confused and foul, so that the heavenly power is, as it were, oppressed. Therefore they say that this is the reason why precious stones more than anything else have wonderful powers" (60—61). While the "seven kinds of metals have their forms from the seven planets of the lower spheres" (168).

Hortulanus: "the stone is divided into two principle parts by the magistry, into a superior part which ascends above and into an inferior part which remains below fixed and clear. And these two parts moreover are concordant in their virtue since the inferior part is earth which is called nurse and ferment, and the superior part is the spirit which quickens the whole stone and raises it up.

"Wherfore separation made, and conjunction celebrated, many miracles are effected."

Burckhardt: "This refers to the reciprocal dependence of the active and the passive . . . essential form cannot be manifested without passive materia. The efficacy of the spiritual power depends on the preparedness of the human 'container' and vice versa. . . . 'Above' and 'below' are thus related to this one thing and complement one another in its regard".

Schumaker: "There are corresponding planes in various levels of creation, hence it is safe to draw analogies between macrocosm and microcosm, the mineral kingdom and the human, animal and vegetable kingdoms etc".

Needham: "the whole affirmation looks remarkably like the doctrine that extreme of Yang generates Yin, and vice versa".

On # Hortulanus: "our stone, which was created by God, was born and came forth from a confused mass, containing in itself all the elements-and hence our stone was born by this single miracle".

Trithemius: "Is it not true that all things flow from one thing, from the goodness of the One, and that whatever is joined to Unity cannot be diverse, but rather fructifies by means of the simplicity and adaptability of the One?" "What is born from Unity? Is it not the ternary? Take note: Unity is unmixed, the binary is compounded, and the ternary is reduced to the simplicity of Unity. I, Trithemius, am not of three minds, but persist in a single integrated mind taking pleasure in the ternary, which gives birth to a marvelous offspring" (Bran).

Burckhardt: "the undivided, invisible Light of the unconditioned One is refracted into multiplicity by the prism of the Spirit". As the Spirit contemplates the Unity without full comprehension "it manifests the 'many-sided' All, just as a lens transmits the light it receives as a bundle of rays".

Schumaker: As God is one, all created objects come from one thing, an undifferentiated primal matter.

On #4 Hortulanus: "As one animal naturally generates more animals similar to itself, so the Sun artificially generates Sun by the power of multiplication of . . . the stone. . . . in this artificial generation it is necessary that the Sun have a suitable receptacle, consonant with itself, for its sperm and its tincture, and this is the Luna of the philosophers."

Redgrove: Sun and Moon "probably stand for Spirit and Matter respectively, not gold and silver".

Burckhardt: Sun "is the spirit (nous), while the moon is the soul (psyche)".

Schumaker: "If the moon is associated with water, as because of its 'moisture' [as] was usual, and the sun with fire, the prima materia is understood to have been generated by fire, born of water, brought down from the sky by wind, and nourished by earth".

On #5 Albertus Magnus: by this Hermes "means the levigatio [making light weight] of the material, raising it to the properties of Air. And why he says the wind carries the material [of the stone] in its belly is that, when the material is placed in an alembic-which is a vessel made like those in which rosewater is prepared-then by evapouration it is rendered subtle and is raised towards the properties of Air . . . And there distills and issues from the mouth of the alembic a watery or oily liquor with all the powers of the elements" (17). In metals the moisture is not separated from the dryness, but is dissolved in it; and being so dissolved, it moves about there as if it had been swallowed by the Earth and were moving about in its bowels. And on this account Hermes said 'The mother of metal is Earth that carries it in her belly'".

Hortulanus: "It is plain that wind is air, and air is life, and life is spirit . . . And thus it is necessary that the wind should bear the whole stone. . . . [However] our stone without the ferment of the earth will never come to the effect, which ferment is called food."

Trithemius: "the wind carries its seed in her belly".

Maier: By "the wind carried him in its belly" Hermes means "'He, whose father is the Sun, and whose mother is the Moon, will be carried before he is born, by wind and vapour, just as a flying bird is carried by air'. From the vapours of winds, which are nothing else but wind in motion, water proceeds, when condensed, and from that water, mixed with earth, all minerals and metals arise". The substance carried by the wind is "in chemical respect, the sulphur, which is carried in mercury". Lull says "'The stone is the fire, carried in the belly of the air'. In physical respect it is the unborn child that will soon be born". To be clearer, "'All mercury is composed of vapours, that is to say of water, which the earth raises along with it into the thin air, and of earth, which the air compels to return into watery earth or earthy water." As the elements contained within are each reduced to a watery condition, they either follow the volatile elements upward as in common mercury, or they stay below with the solid elements as in philosophical Mercury "and in the solid metals". So "Mercury is the wind which receives the sulphur . . . as the unripe fruit from the mothers womb, or from the ashes of the burnt mother's body and takes it to a place where it may ripen".

Ripley says "our child shall be born in the air, that is the belly of the wind" [de Jong 1969: 55–7.] Maier (2nd Comment) on "The earth is its nurse": Food changes into the substance of the eater and is then assimilated. "This harmony dominates the whole of nature, for the like enjoys the like".

The same happens in the Work and Nature "just as is the growth of the child in the mother's womb. So also a father, a mother and a nurse have been attributed to the philosophical child . . . it comes into being from the twofold seed and then grows as an embryo does". As a woman must moderate her diet to avoid miscarriage, "in the same way one must set about philosophical work with moderation". The Seeds also have to be united. "Philosophers say that the one comes from the East and the other from the West and become one; what does this mean but combining in a retort, a moderate temperature and nourishment?" "One may wonder why the earth is referred to as the nurse of the philosophic child, since barreness and dry-ness are the main properties of the element earth". The answer is that not the element, but the whole Earth is meant. "It is the nurse of Heaven not because it resolves, washes and moistens the foetus, but because it coagulates, fastens and colours the latter and changes it into sap and blood . . . The Earth contains a wonderful juice which changes the nature of the one who feeds on it, as Romulus is believed to have been changed by the wolf's milk into a bellicose individual" [de Jong 1969: 63—5.]

Burckhardt: "The wind which carries the spiritual germ in its body, is the vital breath". Vital breath is the substance of the realm between heaven and earth, it "is also Quicksilver which contains the germ of gold in a liquid state". The earth is "the body, as an inward reality".

On #6 Burckhardt: the word talisman is derived from Telesma. Talismans work by corresponding to their prototype, and by making a "'condensation', on the subtle plane, of a spiritual state. This explains the similarity between the talisman, as the bearer of an invisible influence, and the alchemical elixir, as the 'ferment' of metallic transformation".

On #7 Hortulanus: The stone is perfect and complete if it is turned into earth "that is if the soul of the stone itself. . . . is turned into earth, namely of the stone and is fixed so that the whole substance of the stone becomes one with its nurse, namely the earth, and the whole stone is converted to ferment."

Trithemius: it is the seed from #5 that must be cast upon the earth.

Bacstrom: "Process-First Distillation".

Burckhardt: "when the Spirit is 'embodied', the volatile becomes fixed".

Schumaker: if the prime matter is to be used it must be fixed into a substance "capable of being handled".

On #7a Hortulanus: "You will separate, that is, you will dissolve, because solution is separation of parts."

Burkhardt: The separation "means the 'extraction' of the soul from the body".

Schumaker "Since the volatile principle is fire—or sometimes, air-stability is produced by its removal. Or, alternatively but less probably, the earth is impurity ('the gross') and a purified fire ('the subtle') is what is wanted.

On #8 Albertus Magnus: In intending to teach the operations of alchemy Hermes says the stone "'ascends to heaven' when by roasting and calcination it takes on the properties of Fire; for alchemists mean by calcinatio the reduction of material to powder by burning and roasting. And the material 'again descends from heaven to earth' when it takes on the properties of Earth by inhumatio, for inhumation revives and nourishes what was previously killed by calcination".

Hortulanus: "And now he deals with multiplication [of the stone]." "Although our stone is divided in the first operation into four parts . . . there are really two principle parts". The ascending, non fixed, and the earth or ferment. "It is necessary to have a large quantity of this non fixed part and to give it to the stone which has been made thoroughly clean from dirt. . . . until the entire stone is borne above by the virtue of the spirit."

"Afterwards it is necessary to incerate the same stone . . . with the oil that was extracted in the first operation, which oil is called the water of the stone." Roast or boil by sublimation until the "entire stone descends . . . and remains fixed and fluent". "That which is coporeal is made spiritual by sublimation, and that which is spiritual is made corporeal by descension".

Trithemius: "When the ternary has at last returned to itself it may, by an inner disposition and great delight, ascend from the earth to heaven, thereby receiving both superior and inferior power; thus will it be made powerful and glorious in the clarity of Unity, demonstrate its ability to bring forth every number, and put to flight all obscurity".

Bacstrom: "Last Digestion". "The Azoth ascends from the Earth, from the bottom of the Glass, and redescends in Veins and drops into the Earth and by this continual circulation the Azoth is more and more subtilised, Volatilizes Sol and carries the volatilized Solar atoms along with it and thereby becomes a Solar Azoth, i.e. our third and genuine Sophic Mercury". The circulation must continue until "it ceases of itself, and the Earth has sucked it all in, when it becomes the black pitchy matter, the Toad [the substances in the alchemical retort and also the lower elements in the body of man—Hall], which denotes complete putrifaction or Death of the compound".

Read, suggests this section describes the use of a kerotakis, in which metals are suspended and subject to the action of gasses released from substances heated in the base, and from their condensation and circulation.

Burckhardt: "dissolution of consciousness from all formal 'coagulations' is followed by the 'crystalisation' of the Spirit, so that active and passive are perfectly united."

Schumaker: "Separate the volatile part of the substance by vaporization but continue heating until the vapour reunites with the parent body, whereupon you will have obtained the Stone".

On # Trithemius: When the ternary has returned to Unity cleansed of all impurities "the mind understands without contradiction all the mysteries of the excellently arranged arcanum".

Bacstrom: the black matter becomes White and Red. The Red "having been carried to perfection, medicinaly and for Metals" is capable of supporting complete mental and physical health, and provides "ample means, in finitum multiplicable to be benevolent and charitable, without any dimunation of our inexhaustable resources, therefore well may it be called the Glory of the whole World". Contemplation and study of the Philosopher's Stone ("L. P.") elevates the mind to God.

"The Philosophers say with great Truth, that the L.P. either finds a good man or makes one". "By invigorating the Organs the Soul makes use of for communicating with exterior objects, the Soul must aquire greater powers, not only for conception but also for retention". If we pray and have faith "all Obscurity must vanish of course".

Burckhardt: "Thus the light of the Spirit becomes constant. [and] ignorance, deception, uncertainty, doubt and foolishness will be removed from consciousness".

On # Trithemius: The Philosopher's Stone is another name for the 'one thing', and is able to "conquer every subtile thing and to penetrate every solid". "This very noble virtue . . . consists of maximal fortitude, touching everything with its desirable excellence".

Bacstrom: "The L.P. does possess all the Powers concealed in Nature, not for destruction but for exhaltation and regeneration of matter, in the three Departments of Nature". "It refixes the most subtil Oxygen into its own firey Nature". The power increases "in a tenfold ratio, at every multiplication". So it can penetrate Gold and Silver, and fix mercury, Crystals and Glass Fluxes.

Burckhardt: "Alchemical fixation is nevertheless more inward . . . Through its union with the spirit bodily consciousness itself becomes a fine and penetrating power". He quotes Jabir "The body becomes a spirit, and takes on . . . fineness, lightness, extensibility, coloration . . . The spirit . . . becomes a body and aquires the latter's resistance to fire, immobility and duration. From both bodies a light substance is born, which. precisely takes up a middle position between the two extremes".

Schumaker: The product of the distillation and reunion will "dominate less solid substances, but because of its own subtlety it will 'penetrate' and hence dominate, other solid things less pure and quasi-spiritual than itself".

On # Burckhardt: "the little world is created according to the prototype of the great world", when the human realises their original nature is the image of God.

Schumaker: "The alchemical operation is a paradigm of the creative process. We may note the sexual overtones of what has preceeded"

On #12 Burckhardt: "In the Arabic text this is: "This way is traversed by the sages".

On # Hortulanus: "He here teaches in an occult manner the things from which the stone is made." "the stone is called perfect because it has in itself the nature of minerals, of vegetables and of animals.

For the stone is three and one, tripple and single, having four natures. . . . and three colours, namely black, white and red. It is also called the grain of corn because unless it shall have died, it remains itself alone. And if it shall have died . . . it bears much fruit when it is in conjunction . . ."

Newton: "on account of this art Mercurius is called thrice greatest, having three parts of the philosophy of the whole world, since he signifies the Mercury of the philosophers. . . . and has dominion in the mineral kingdom, the vegetable kingdom, and the animal kingdom".

Bacstrom: the wisdom of the world (?) is hidden in "Chiram and its Use". Hermes "signifies a Serpent, and the Serpent used to be an Emblem of Knowledge or Wisdom."

Burckhardt: "The three parts of wisdom correspond to the three great divisions of the universe, namely, the spiritual, psychic and corporeal realms, whose symbols are heaven, air and earth".

Schumaker: "The usual explanation of Tristmegistus. is that Hermes was the greatest philosopher, the greatest priest, and the greatest king".

GENERAL

Trithemius: "our philosophy is celestial, not worldly, in order that we may faithfuly behold, by means of a direct intuition of the mind through faith and knowledge, that principle which we call God. . . ."

Trithemius: "Study generates knowledge; knowledge prepares love; love, similarity; similarity, communion; communion, virtue; virtue, dignity; dignity, power; and power performs the miracle".

Newton "Inferior and superior, fixed and volatile, sulphur and quicksilver have a similar nature and are one thing, like man and wife. For they differ from one another only by degree of digestion and maturity. Sulphur is mature quicksilver, and quicksilver is immature sulphur: and on account of this affinity they unite like male and female, and they act on each other, and through that action they are mutually transmuted into each other and procreate a more noble offspring to accomplish the miracles of this one thing". "And just as all things were created from one Chaos by the design of one God, so in our art all things . . . are born from this one thing which is our Chaos, by the design of the Artificer and the skilful adaptation of things. And the generation of this is similar to the human, truly from a father and mother".

Blavatsky: the mysterious thing "is the universal, magical agent, the astral light, which in the correlations of its forces furnishes the alkahest, the philosopher's stone, and the elixir of life.

Hermetic philosophy names it Azoth, the soul of the world, the celestial virgin, the great Magnes, etc" It appears to be that which gives organisation ("the maze of force-correlations"), and form i.e. the perfect geometry of snowflakes.

Sherwood Taylor: "the operation of the Sun. was carried out by a 'spirit', universal, the source of all things, having the power of perfecting them. Its virtue is integral [# 6a] (ie having the power to convert the diverse into a single substance), if it be turned into earth (ie. solidified). This conveyed that the Stone was to be a solidified pneuma. Pneuma was the link between earth and heaven, having the virtue of the celestial and subterranean regions-the power of the whole cosmos from the fixed stars to the centre of the earth. It overcomes every nature and penetrates every solid. It is the source of the whole world and so it can be the means of changing things in a wonderful way.

The three parts of the philosophy of the whole world are presumably of the celestial, terrestrial, and subterranean regions".

Shah: The table is "the same as the Sufi dictum . . . 'Man is the microcosm, creation the macrocosm—the unity. All comes from One. By the joining of the power of contemplation all can be attained.

This essence must be separated from the body first, then combined with the body. This is the Work. Start with yourself, end with all. Before man, beyond man, transformation'".

A COMMENTARY OF IBN UMAIL

HERMUS said the secret of everything and the life of everything is Water. . . . This water becomes in wheat, ferment; in the vine, wine; in the olive, olive oil. . . . The begining of the child is from water. . . . Regarding this spiritual water and the sanctified and thirsty earth, HERMUS the great, crowned with the glorious wisdom and the sublime sciences, said [#1] Truth it is, indubitable, certain and correct, [#2] that the High is from the Low and the Low is from the High. They bring about wonders through the one, just as things are produced from that one essence by a single preparation. Later by his statement [#4] Its father is the Sun and its mother the Moon he meant their male and their female. They are the two birds which are linked together in the pictures given regarding the beginning of the operation, and from them the spiritual tinctures are produced. And similarly they are at the end of the operation. Later in his statement [#7 ?] the subtle is more honourable than the gross, he means by the subtle the divine spiritual water; and by the gross the earthly body. As for his later statement [#8] with gentleness and wisdom it will ascend from the earth to the sky, and will take fire from the higher lights, he means by this the distillation and the raising of the water into the air. As for his later statement [#8a] It will descend to the earth, containing the strength of the high and the low, he means by this the breathing in (istinshaq) of the air, and the taking of the spirit from it, and its subsequent elevation to the highest degree of heat, and it is the Fire, and the low is the body, and its content of the controlling earthly power which imparts the colours. For there lie in it those higher powers, as well as the earthly powers which were submerged in it.

The natural operation and decay causes it to be manifest, and hence the strength of the earth, and of the air, and of the higher fire passed in to it. Later he said [#9] it will overcome the high and the low because it in it is found the light of lights: and consequently the darkness will flee from it. [See Stapleton et al. p 74, 81.]

Appendix

Translation from Roger Bacon's edition of Secretum Secretorum made c 1445

1. Trouth hath hym so, and it is no doubt,
2. that the lover is to the heigher, and the heigher to the lower aunsweren.
   The worcher forsoth of all myracles is the one and sool God, of and fro Whom Cometh all meruelous operacions.
3. So all thynges were created of o soole substance, and of o soole disposicion,
4. the fader wherof is the sone, and the moone moder,
5. that brought hym forth by blast or aier in the wombe, the erthe taken fro it,
6. to whom is seid the increat fader, tresour of myracles, and yever of vertues.
7. Of fire is made erthe.
7a. Depart the erthe fro the fire, for the sotiller is worthier than the more grosse, and the thynne thynge than the thik. This most be do wisely and discretly.
8. It ascendith fro the erth into the heven, and falleth fro heven to the erthe, and therof sleith the higher and the lower vertue.
9. And yf it lordship in the lower and in the heigher, and thow shalt lordship aboue and beneth, which forsoth is the light of lightes, and therfor fro the wolle fle all derknesse.
10. The higher vertue ouer-cometh all, for sothe all thynne thyng doth in dense thynges.
11a. After the disposicion of the more world rynneth this worchyng.
11. And for this prophetisyng of the trynyte of God Hermogenes it called Triplex, trebil in philosophie, as Aristotle seith.

[See Manzalaoui 1977: 65–6.]

Translation of same source, made c. 1485.

APPENDIX

1. The trwthe is so, and that it is no dowght,

2. that lower thyngis to hyer thyng, and hyer to lower be correspondent. But the Werker of myraclis is on Godde alone, fro Home descendyth euiry meruulus werk.

3. And so alle thyngis be creat of one only substauns, be an only dysposicion,

4. of home the fadyr is the sonne, and the mone the modyr,

5. qwyche bar her be the wedyr in the wombe. The erthe is priuyd fro her-to.

6. This is clepyd or seyd the fadyr of enchauntmentis, tresur of myracclys, the yessuer of vertuys.

7. Be a lytil it is made erthe.

8. Depart that qwyche is erthly fro that qwyche is fi Fry, for that qwyche is sotel is mor wurthy han that qwyche is grose, and that rar, porous, or lyght, is mor bettyr than qwiche is thyk of substauns. This is done wyseli or dyscretly.

9. It ascendyth fro the erth in-to heuyn and fallyth fro heuyn in-to erth, and ther-of it sleth the ouyr vertu and the nedyr vertu, so it hath lorchyp in the lowe thyngis and hye thingis,

10. and thu lordschyppist vppeward and downward, and with the is the lyght of lyghtys. And for that alle derkness schal fle fro the.

11. The ovyr vetu ouircomyth alle, for euiry rar rhyng werkyth in to euiry thyk thyng.

12. And aftyr the dysposicion of the mor world rennyth thys werking.

13. And for that Hermogines is clepyd threfold in filosophye, and of the mer-uellys of he world.

[See Manzalaoui 1977: 174–5]

Bibliography

Albertus Magnus, Book of Minerals, trans D. Wyckoff, OUP, 1967.

Anon Meditations on the Tarot. Amity House, 1985 pp 21–6 Brann, N.L. "George Ripley and the Abbot Trithemius", Ambix, vol 26, no 3, pp 212–220, 1979.

Blavatsky, H.P. Isis Unveiled. Theosophical University Press, pp 507–14 1972.

Burckhardt, T. Alchemy. Stuart and Watkins, London pp 196–201 1967.

Davis, Tenny L. "The Emerald Tablet of Hermes Tristmegistus: Three Latin versions which were current among later Alchemists", Journal of Chemical Education, Vol.3, no.8, pp 863–75, 1926.

de Jong, H.M.E. Michael Maiers's Atlanta Fugiens: Sources of an alchemical Book of Emblems, E. J. Brill, Leiden 1969.

Dobbs, B.J. "Newton's Commentary on the Emerald Tablet of Hermes Trismegistus" in Merkel, I and Debus A.G. Hermeticism and the Renaissance. Folger, Washington 1988.

Fulcanelli. Les Demeures Philosophales. Jean Jacques Pavert, Paris, 1964.

Hall, M.P. The Secret Teachings of all Ages. Philosophical Research, L.A. 1977 pp CLVII–CLVIII.

Holmyard, E.J. "The Emerald Table" Nature, Oct 6th pp 525–6, 1929.

Holmyard, E.J. Alchemy, Pelican, Harmondsworth 1957 pp 95–8.

Linden, Stanton J. ed. "The Mirror of Alchimy Composed by the Thrice-Famous and Learned Fryer Roger Bacon (1597), Garland, NY, 1992.

Manzalaoui, M.A. Secretum Secretorum: Nine English Versions, Early English Text Society, Oxford University Press, 1977.

Needham, J. Science and Civilisation in China vol 5, part 4: Spagyrical discovery and invention: Apparatus, Theories and gifts. CUP, 1980.

Read, John Prelude to Chemistry, G Bell, London, 1939 pp15, 51–5.

Redgrove, S. Alchemy: Ancient and Modem. William Rider, London, 1922. pp 40–42.

BIBLIOGRAPHY

Sadoul, J. Alchemists and Gold. G.P. Putnams, NY pp 25–6 1972.

Schumaker, Wayne. The Occult Sciences in the Renaissance. University of California, Berkely pp 179–80 1972.

Shah, Idres. The Sufis. Octagon, London p 198 1977.

Sherwood Taylor, F. The Alchemists. Paladin, pp 77–8 1976.

Stapleton, H.E., Lewis, G.L, Sherwood Taylor, F. "The sayings of Hermes quoted in the Ma Al-Waraqi of Ibn Umail." Ambix, vol 3, pp 69–90, 1949.

Steele, R. and Singer, D.W. "The Emerald Table". Proceedings of the Royal Society of Medicine vol 21, 1928.

THE KYBALION

Contents

CONTENTS

To

HERMES TRISMEGISTUS,
known by the ancient Egyptians as
"THE GREAT GREAT,"
and
"MASTER OF MASTERS,"
this little volume of Hermetic Teachings is reverently dedicated.

Foreword

In 1908, a book was published that has gone on to sell millions of copies and influence countless readers. Titled *The Kybalion,* this book was said to contain the teachings of Hermeticism, that is, the teachings of Hermes Trismegistus, the thrice-greatest Hermes, a god connected to Hermes in the Greek tradition and Thoth in the Egyptian tradition.

The author of *The Kybalion?* The book was published by The Yogi Publication Society of Chicago under the pseudonym the Three Initiates. Who are the Three Initiates? There have been many guesses and much speculation over the years, but most modern scholars believe that the book was authored by William Walker Atkinson, a popular New Thought teacher around the early twentieth century. Atkinson founded and owned The Yogi Publication Society, and the books they published were mostly (if not all) by Atkinson, often using pseudonyms such as Yogi Ramacharaka, Swami Bhakta Vishita, Swami Panchadasi, Theron Q. Dumont, Magus Incognito, and others. There is some speculation that he was aided in writing *The Kybalion* by metaphysical teachers of the time, including Paul Foster Case, Claude Alexander, and Elias Gewurz. In my opinion, as a long-time student of *The Kybalion,* I believe that the book was indeed written by Atkinson, and I believe he wrote it by himself.

In any case, authorship of the book is less important than the material the book contains. The book contains seven basic principles, which were said to have been passed down from teacher to student for centuries. The seven transformative principles, or laws, are:

Mentalism: Everything is mind
Correspondence: As above, so below
Vibration: Everything vibrates with movement
Polarity: Everything is dual
Rhythm: Ebb and flow
Cause and Effect: Every cause has an effect, every effect has a cause
Gender: Everything has masculine and feminine energy

These principles mirrored the work of popular New Thought teachers at the time, including Thomas Troward, Emma Curtis Hopkins, and Ralph Waldo Trine. The book arrived at a time when readers were open to sacred teachings from around the world, discovering books like the Bhagavad Gita, the Upanishads, and other works that were being newly studied in English.

The seven principles create a bridge between ancient mystical teachings and the teachings from the Transcendentalist movement happening in New England. It's no wonder that readers devoured the teaching in this book—deep, essential truth-teaching put into clear language that made the ideas accessible. *The Kybalion* went on to influence New Thought teachers such as Ernest Holmes and Emmet Fox, as well as modern-day teachers such as Rhonda Byrne and Wayne Dyer.

The language of *The Kybalion* is one of secret teachings that the reader has discovered, at the exact right moment, when the reader was ready for them. As the book states, "The Principles of Truth are Seven; he who knows these, understandingly, possess the Magic Key before whose touch all Doors of the Temple fly open."

I first discovered *The Kybalion* back in the 1980s, a little blue hardcover with gold type on the cover, found in a small metaphysical bookstore. I had no idea what a "kybalion" was, or who the Three Initiates were, but something about the book called to me. Maybe it was true that I was ready for those particular teachings. I began the book and could almost feel the wisdom of it become imprinted in my mind. It made a difference in my thinking and my actions. Finally, a book of deep spiritual wisdom that I could dive into and begin using in my life immediately. Truthfully, when I read the book that first time, I didn't care who wrote it. I only cared if the material was true or not, and for me, it contained Truth.

Since that first time, I've read the book many times over the years. When I read other books, published after *The Kybalion* was in 1908, I can see the influence of this book in those. Also, learning these universal seven principles allowed me to have a language to understand other spiritual teachings and wisdom.

If, like me, you have studied *The Kybalion* before, then you already know the delicious reading that is ahead of you. And I'm glad you have a copy of our Essential Wisdom Library edition, which contains the complete, original text.

If, however, you are new to *The Kybalion,* I am excited for you. Technically you can dip into the book at any point, start reading any of the principles in any order. I would suggest, though, that you begin at the first page and read through it start to finish. Jump in and see where this journey takes you.

The mere fact that you are reading a copy of *The Kybalion* tells me that there is something in this book that you need, and you need it right now. It has an answer for you, maybe more than one. And if you read with an open mind and with eagerness, that answer will make itself known to you. It may pop out at you immediately, or you may need to search for it, but it's there. It absolutely is there. . . .

—JOEL FOTINOS
New York, 2020

Introduction

We take great pleasure in presenting to the attention of students and investigators of the Secret Doctrines this little work based upon the world-old Hermetic Teachings. There has been so little written upon this subject, notwithstanding the countless references to the Teachings in the many works upon occultism, that the many earnest searchers after the Arcane Truths will doubtless welcome the appearance of the present volume.

The purpose of this work is not the enunciation of any special philosophy or doctrine, but rather is to give to the students a statement of the Truth that will serve to reconcile the many bits of occult knowledge that they may have acquired, but which are apparently opposed to each other and which often serve to discourage and disgust the beginner in the study. Our intent is not to erect a new Temple of Knowledge, but rather to place in the hands of the student a Master-Key with which he may open the many inner doors in the Temple of Mystery through the main portals he has already entered.

There is no portion of the occult teachings possessed by the world which have been so closely guarded as the fragments of the Hermetic Teachings which have come down to us over the tens of centuries which have elapsed since the lifetime of its great founder, Hermes Trismegistus, the "scribe of the gods," who dwelt in old Egypt in the days when the present race of men was in its infancy. Contemporary with Abraham, and, if the legends be true, an instructor of that venerable sage, Hermes was, and is, the Great Central Sun of Occultism, whose rays have served to illumine the countless teachings which have been promulgated since his time. All the fundamental and basic teachings embedded in the esoteric teachings of every race may be traced back to Hermes. Even the most ancient teachings of India undoubtedly have their roots in the original Hermetic Teachings.

From the land of the Ganges many advanced occultists wandered to the land of Egypt, and sat at the feet of the Master. From him they obtained the Master-Key which explained and reconciled their divergent views, and thus the Secret Doctrine was firmly established. From other lands also came the learned ones, all of whom regarded Hermes as the Master of Masters, and his influence was so great that in spite of the many wanderings from the path on the part of the centuries of teachers in these different lands, there may still be found a certain basic resemblance and correspondence which underlies the many and often quite divergent theories entertained and taught by the occultists of these different lands today. The student of Comparative Religions will be able to perceive the influence of the Hermetic Teachings in every religion worthy of the name, now known to man, whether it be a dead religion or one in full vigor in our own times. There is always a certain correspondence in spite of the contradictory features, and the Hermetic Teachings act as the Great Reconciler.

The lifework of Hermes seems to have been in the direction of planting the great Seed-Truth which has grown and blossomed in so many strange forms, rather than to establish a school of philosophy which would dominate the world's thought. But, nevertheless, the original truths taught by him have been kept intact in their original purity by a few men in each age, who, refusing great numbers of half-developed students and followers, followed the Hermetic custom and reserved their truth for the few who were ready to comprehend and master it. From lip to ear the truth has been handed down among the few. There have always been a few Initiates in each generation, in the various lands of the earth, who kept alive the sacred flame of the Hermetic Teachings, and such have always been willing to use their lamps to re-light the lesser lamps of the outside world, when the light of truth grew dim, and clouded by reason of neglect, and when the wicks became clogged with foreign matter. There were always a few to tend faithfully the altar of the Truth, upon which was kept alight the Perpetual Lamp of Wisdom. These men devoted their lives to the labor of love which the poet has so well stated in his lines:

"O, let not the flame die out! Cherished age after age in its dark cavern—in its holy temples cherished. Fed by pure ministers of love—let not the flame die out!"

These men have never sought popular approval, nor numbers of followers. They are indifferent to these things, for they know how few there are in each generation who are ready for the truth, or who would recognize it if it were presented to them. They reserve the "strong meat for men," while others furnish the "milk for babes." They reserve their pearls of wisdom for the few elect, who recognize their value and who wear them in their crowns, instead of casting them before the materialistic vulgar swine, who would trample them in the mud and mix them with their disgusting mental food. But still these men have never forgotten or overlooked the original teachings of Hermes, regarding the passing on of the words of truth to those ready to receive it, which teaching is stated in *The Kybalion* as follows: "Where fall the footsteps of the Master, the ears of those ready for his Teaching open wide." And again: "When the ears of the student are ready to hear, then cometh the lips to fill them with wisdom." But their customary attitude has always been strictly in accordance with the other Hermetic aphorism, also in *The Kybalion*: "The lips of Wisdom are closed, except to the ears of Understanding."

There are those who have criticised this attitude of the Hermetists, and who have claimed that they did not manifest the proper spirit in their policy of seclusion and reticence. But a moment's glance back over the pages of history will show the wisdom of the Masters, who knew the folly of attempting to teach to the world that which it was neither ready or willing to receive. The Hermetists have never sought to be martyrs, and have, instead, sat silently aside with a pitying smile on their closed lips, while the "heathen raged noisily about them" in their customary amusement of putting to death and torture the honest but misguided enthusiasts who imagined that they could force upon a race of barbarians the truth capable of being understood only by the elect who had advanced along The Path.

And the spirit of persecution has not as yet died out in the land. There are certain Hermetic Teachings, which, if publicly promulgated, would bring down upon the teachers a great cry of scorn and revilement from the multitude, who would again raise the cry of "Crucify! Crucify."

In this little work we have endeavored to give you an idea of the fundamental teachings of *The Kybalion*, striving to give you the working Principles, leaving you to apply them yourselves, rather than attempting to work out the teaching in detail. If you are a true student, you will be able to work out and apply these Principles—if not, then you must develop yourself into one, for otherwise the Hermetic Teachings will be as "words, words, words" to you.

The Three Initiates

1

The Hermetic Philosophy

"The lips of wisdom are closed, except to the ears of Understanding."

—THE KYBALION

From old Egypt have come the fundamental esoteric and occult teachings which have so strongly influenced the philosophies of all races, nations and peoples, for several thousand years. Egypt, the home of the Pyramids and the Sphinx, was the birthplace of the Hidden Wisdom and Mystic Teachings. From her Secret Doctrine all nations have borrowed. India, Persia, Chaldea, Medea, China, Japan, Assyria, ancient Greece and Rome, and other ancient countries partook liberally at the feast of knowledge which the Hierophants and Masters of the Land of Isis so freely provided for those who came prepared to partake of the great store of Mystic and Occult Lore which the masterminds of that ancient land had gathered together.

In ancient Egypt dwelt the great Adepts and Masters who have never been surpassed, and who seldom have been equaled, during the centuries that have taken their processional flight since the days of the Great Hermes. In Egypt was located the Great Lodge of Lodges of the Mystics. At the doors of her Temples entered the Neophytes who afterward, as Hierophants, Adepts, and Masters, traveled to the four corners of the earth, carrying with them the precious knowledge which they were ready, anxious, and willing to pass on to those who were ready to receive the same. All students of the Occult recognize the debt that they owe to these venerable Masters of that ancient land.

But among these great Masters of Ancient Egypt there once dwelt one of whom Masters hailed as "The Master of Masters." This man, if "man" indeed he was, dwelt in Egypt in the earliest days. He was known as Hermes Trismegistus. He was the father of the Occult Wisdom; the founder of Astrology; the discoverer of Alchemy. The details of his life story are lost to history, owing to the lapse of the years, though several of the ancient countries disputed with each other in their claims to the honor of having furnished his birthplace—and this thousands of years ago. The date of his sojourn in Egypt, in that his last incarnation on this planet, is not now known, but it has been fixed at the early days of the oldest dynasties of Egypt—long before the days of Moses. The best authorities regard him as a contemporary of Abraham, and some of the Jewish traditions go so far as to claim that Abraham acquired a portion of his mystic knowledge from Hermes himself.

As the years rolled by after his passing from this plane of life (tradition recording that he lived three hundred years in the flesh), the Egyptians deified Hermes, and made him one of their gods, under the name of Thoth. Years after, the people of Ancient Greece also made him one of their many gods—calling him "Hermes, the god of Wisdom." The Egyptians revered his memory for many centuries—yes, tens of centuries—calling him "the Scribe of the Gods," and bestowing upon him, distinctively, his ancient title, "Trismegistus," which means "the thrice-great"; "the great-great"; "the greatest-great"; etc. In all the ancient lands, the name of Hermes Trismegistus was revered, the name being synonymous with the "Fount of Wisdom."

Even to this day, we use the term "hermetic" in the sense of "secret"; "sealed so that nothing can escape"; etc., and this by reason of the fact that the followers of Hermes always observed the principle of secrecy in their teachings. They did not believe in "casting pearls before swine," but rather held to the teaching "milk for babes; meat for strong men," both of which maxims are familiar to readers of the Christian scriptures, but both of which had been used by the Egyptians for centuries before the Christian era.

And this policy of careful dissemination of the truth has always characterized the Hermetics, even unto the present day. The Hermetic Teachings are to be found in all lands, among all religions, but never identified with any particular country, nor with any particular religious sect. This because of the warning of the ancient teachers against allowing the Secret Doctrine to become crystallized into a creed. The wisdom of this caution is apparent to all students of history. The ancient occultism of India and Persia degenerated, and was largely lost, owing to the fact that the teachers became priests, and so mixed theology with the philosophy, the result being that the occultism of India and Persia has been gradually lost amidst the mass of religious superstition, cults, creeds and "gods." So it was with Ancient Greece and Rome. So it was with the Hermetic Teachings of the Gnostics and Early Christians, which were lost at the time of Constantine, whose iron hand smothered philosophy with the blanket of theology, losing to the Christian Church that which was its very essence and spirit, and causing it to grope throughout several centuries before it found the way back to its ancient faith, the indications apparent to all careful observers in this Twentieth Century being that the Church is now struggling to get back to its ancient mystic teachings.

But there were always a few faithful souls who kept alive the Flame, tending it carefully, and not allowing its light to become extinguished. And thanks to these staunch hearts, and fearless minds, we have the truth still with us. But it is not found in books, to any great extent. It has been passed along from Master to Student; from Initiate to Hierophant; from lip to ear. When it was written down at all, its meaning was veiled in terms of alchemy and astrology, so that only those possessing the key could read it aright. This was made necessary in order to avoid the persecutions of the theologians of the Middle Ages, who fought the Secret Doctrine with fire and sword; stake, gibbet and cross. Even to this day there will be found but few reliable books on the Hermetic Philosophy, although there are countless references to it in many books written on various phases of Occultism. And yet, the Hermetic Philosophy is the only Master Key which will open all the doors of the Occult Teachings!

In the early days, there was a compilation of certain Basic Hermetic Doctrines, passed on from teacher to student, which was known as "THE KYBALION," the exact significance and meaning of the term having been lost for several centuries. This teaching, however, is known to many to whom it has descended, from mouth to ear, on and on throughout the centuries. Its precepts have never been written down, or printed, so far as we know. It was merely a collection of maxims, axioms, and precepts, which were non-understandable to outsiders, but which were readily understood by students, after the axioms, maxims, and precepts had been explained and exemplified by the Hermetic Initiates to their Neophytes. These teachings really constituted the basic principles of "The Art of Hermetic Alchemy," which, contrary to the general belief, dealt in the mastery of Mental Forces, rather than Material Elements—the Transmutation of one kind of Mental Vibrations into others, instead of the changing of one kind of metal into another. The legends of the "Philosopher's Stone" which would turn base metal into Gold, was an allegory relating to Hermetic Philosophy, readily understood by all students of true Hermeticism.

In this little book, of which this is the First Lesson, we invite our students to examine into the Hermetic Teachings, as set forth in THE KYBALION, and as explained by ourselves, humble students of the Teachings, who, while bearing the title of Initiates, are still students at the feet of HERMES, the Master. We herein give you many of the maxims, axioms and precepts of THE KYBALION, accompanied by explanations and illustrations which we deem likely to render the teachings more easily comprehended by the modern student, particularly as the original text is purposely veiled in obscure terms.

The original maxims, axioms, and precepts of "THE KY-BALION" are printed herein, in quotation marks, the proper credit being given. Our own work is printed in the regular way, in the body of the work. We trust that the many students to whom we now offer this little work will derive as much benefit from the study of its pages as have the many who have gone on before, treading the same Path to Mastery throughout the centuries that have passed since the times of HERMES TRISMEGISTUS—the Master of Masters—the Great-Great. In the words of "THE KYBALION":

> *"Where fall the footsteps of the Master, the ears of those ready for his Teaching open wide."*
>
> —THE KYBALION

> *"When the ears of the student are ready to hear, then cometh the lips to fill them with Wisdom."*
>
> —THE KYBALION

So that according to the Teachings, the passage of this book to those ready for the instruction will attract the attention of such as are prepared to receive the Teaching. And, likewise, when the pupil is ready to receive the truth, then will this little book come to him, or her. Such is The Law. The Hermetic Principle of Cause and Effect, in its aspect of The Law of Attraction, will bring lips and ear together—pupil and book in company. So mote it be!

2

The Seven Hermetic Principles

"The Principles of Truth are Seven; he who knows these, understandingly, possesses the Magic Key before whose touch all the Doors of the Temple fly open."

—THE KYBALION

The Seven Hermetic Principles, upon which the entire Hermetic Philosophy is based, are as follows:

1. The Principle of Mentalism
2. The Principle of Correspondence
3. The Principle of Vibration
4. The Principle of Polarity
5. The Principle of Rhythm
6. The Principle of Cause and Effect
7. The Principle of Gender

These Seven Principles will be discussed and explained as we proceed with these lessons. A short explanation of each, however, may as well be given at this point.

1. The Principle of Mentalism

"THE ALL is MIND; the Universe is Mental."
—THE KYBALION

This Principle embodies the truth that "All is Mind." It explains that THE ALL (which is the Substantial Reality underlying all the outward manifestations and appearances which we know under the terms of "The Material Universe"; the "Phenomena of Life"; "Matter"; "Energy"; and, in short, all that is apparent to our material senses) is SPIRIT, which in itself is UNKNOWABLE and UNDEFINABLE, but which may be considered and thought of as A UNIVERSAL, INFINITE, LIVING MIND. It also explains that all the phenomenal world or universe is simply a Mental Creation of THE ALL, subject to the Laws of Created Things, and that the universe, as a whole, and in its parts or units, has its existence in the Mind of THE ALL, in which Mind we "live and move and have our being." This Principle, by establishing the Mental Nature of the Universe, easily explains all of the varied mental and psychic phenomena that occupy such a large portion of the public attention, and which, without such explanation, are non-understandable and defy scientific treatment. An understanding of this great Hermetic Principle of Mentalism enables the individual to readily grasp the laws of the Mental Universe, and to apply the same to his well-being and advancement. The Hermetic Student is enabled to apply intelligently the great Mental Laws, instead of using them in a haphazard manner. With the Master-Key in his possession, the student may unlock the many doors of the mental and psychic temple of knowledge, and enter the same freely and intelligently. This Principle explains the true nature of "Energy," "Power," and "Matter," and why and how all these are subordinate to the Mastery of Mind. One of the old Hermetic Masters wrote, long ages ago: "He who grasps the truth of the Mental Nature of the Universe is well advanced on The Path to Mastery." And these words are as true to-day as at the time they were first written. Without this Master-Key, Mastery is impossible, and the student knocks in vain at the many doors of The Temple.

2. The Principle of Correspondence

"As above, so below; as below, so above."

—THE KYBALION

This Principle embodies the truth that there is always a Correspondence between the laws and phenomena of the various planes of Being and Life. The old Hermetic axiom ran in these words: "As above, so below; as below, so above." And the grasping of this Principle gives one the means of solving many a dark paradox, and hidden secret of Nature. There are planes beyond our knowing, but when we apply the Principle of Correspondence to them we are able to understand much that would otherwise be unknowable to us. This Principle is of universal application and manifestation, on the various planes of the material, mental, and spiritual universe—it is a Universal Law. The ancient Hermetists considered this Principle as one of the most important mental instruments by which man was able to pry aside the obstacles which hid from view the Unknown. Its use even tore aside the Veil of Isis to the extent that a glimpse of the face of the goddess might be caught. Just as a knowledge of the Principles of Geometry enables man to measure distant suns and their movements, while seated in his observatory, so a knowledge of the Principle of Correspondence enables Man to reason intelligently from the Known to the Unknown. Studying the monad, he understands the archangel.

3. The Principle of Vibration

"Nothing rests; everything moves; everything vibrates."
—THE KYBALION

This Principle embodies the truth that "everything is in motion"; "everything vibrates"; "nothing is at rest"; facts which Modern Science endorses, and which each new scientific discovery tends to verify. And yet this Hermetic Principle was enunciated thousands of years ago, by the Masters of Ancient Egypt. This Principle explains that the differences between different manifestations of Matter, Energy, Mind, and even Spirit, result largely from varying rates of Vibration. From THE ALL, which is Pure Spirit, down to the grossest form of Matter, all is in vibration—the higher the vibration, the higher the position in the scale. The vibration of Spirit is at such an infinite rate of intensity and rapidity that it is practically at rest—just as a rapidly moving wheel seems to be motionless. And at the other end of the scale, there are gross forms of matter whose vibrations are so low as to seem at rest. Between these poles, there are millions upon millions of varying degrees of vibration. From corpuscle and electron, atom and molecule, to worlds and universes, everything is in vibratory motion. This is also true on the planes of energy and force (which are but varying degrees of vibration); and also on the mental planes (whose states depend upon vibrations); and even on to the spiritual planes. An understanding of this Principle, with the appropriate formulas, enables Hermetic students to control their own mental vibrations as well as those of others. The Masters also apply this Principle to the conquering of Natural phenomena, in various ways. "He who understands the Principle of Vibration, has grasped the sceptre of power," says one of the old writers.

4. The Principle of Polarity

"Everything is Dual; everything has poles; everything has its pair of opposites; like and unlike are the same; opposites are identical in nature, but different in degree; extremes meet; all truths are but half-truths; all paradoxes may be reconciled."

—THE KYBALION

This Principle embodies the truth that "everything is dual"; "everything has two poles"; "everything has its pair of opposites," all of which were old Hermetic axioms. It explains the old paradoxes, that have perplexed so many, which have been stated as follows: "Thesis and antithesis are identical in nature, but different in degree"; "opposites are the same, differing only in degree"; "the pairs of opposites may be reconciled"; "extremes meet"; "everything is and isn't, at the same time"; "all truths are but half-truths"; "every truth is half-false"; "there are two sides to everything," etc., etc., etc. It explains that in everything there are two poles, or opposite aspects, and that "opposites" are really only the two extremes of the same thing, with many varying degrees between them. To illustrate: Heat and Cold, although "opposites," are really the same thing, the differences consisting merely of degrees of the same thing. Look at your thermometer and see if you can discover where "heat" terminates and "cold" begins! There is no such thing as "absolute heat" or "absolute cold"—the two terms "heat" and "cold" simply indicate varying degrees of the same thing, and that "same thing" which manifests as "heat" and "cold" is merely a form, variety, and rate of Vibration. So "heat" and "cold" are simply the "two poles" of that which we call "Heat"—and the phenomena attendant thereupon are manifestations of the Principle of Polarity. The same Principle manifests in the case of "Light and Darkness," which are the same thing, the difference consisting of varying degrees between the two poles of the phenomena. Where does "darkness" leave off, and "light" begin? What is the difference between "Large and Small"? Between "Hard and Soft"? Between "Black and White"? Between "Sharp and Dull"? Between "Noise and Quiet"? Between "High and Low"? Between "Positive and Negative"? The Principle of Polarity explains these paradoxes, and no other Principle can supersede it. The same Principle operates on the Mental Plane. Let us take a radical and extreme example—that of "Love and Hate," two mental states apparently totally different. And yet there are degrees of Hate and degrees of Love, and a middle point in which we use the terms "Like or Dislike," which shade into each other so gradually that sometimes we are at a loss to know whether we "like" or "dislike" or "neither." And all are simply degrees of the same thing, as you will see if you will but think a moment. And, more than this (and considered of more importance by the Hermetists), it is possible to change the vibrations of Hate to the vibrations of Love, in one's own mind, and in the minds of others. Many of you, who read these lines, have had personal experiences of the involuntary rapid transition from Love to Hate, and the reverse, in your own case and that of others. And you will therefore realize the possibility of this being accomplished by the use of the Will, by means of the Hermetic formulas. "Good and Evil" are but the poles of the same thing, and the Hermetist understands the art of transmuting Evil into Good, by means of an application of the Principle of Polarity. In short, the "Art of Polarization" becomes a phase of "Mental Alchemy" known and practiced by the ancient and modern Hermetic Masters. An understanding of the Principle will enable one to change his own Polarity, as well as that of others, if he will devote the time and study necessary to master the art.

5. The Principle of Rhythm

"Everything flows, out and in; everything has its tides; all things rise and fall; the pendulum-swing manifests in everything; the measure of the swing to the right is the measure of the swing to the left; rhythm compensates."

—THE KYBALION

This Principle embodies the truth that in everything there is manifested a measured motion, to and fro; a flow and inflow; a swing backward and forward; a pendulum-like movement; a tide-like ebb and flow; a high-tide and low-tide; between the two poles which exist in accordance with the Principle of Polarity described a moment ago. There is always an action and a reaction; an advance and a retreat; a rising and a sinking. This is in the affairs of the Universe, suns, worlds, men, animals, mind, energy, and matter. This law is manifest in the creation and destruction of worlds; in the rise and fall of nations; in the life of all things; and finally in the mental states of Man (and it is with this latter that the Hermetists find the understanding of the Principle most important). The Hermetists have grasped this Principle, finding its universal application, and have also discovered certain means to overcome its effects in themselves by the use of the appropriate formulas and methods. They apply the Mental Law of Neutralization. They cannot annul the Principle, or cause it to cease its operation, but they have learned how to escape its effects upon themselves to a certain degree depending upon the Mastery of the Principle. They have learned how to USE it, instead of being USED BY it. In this and similar methods, consist the Art of the Hermetists. The Master of Hermetics polarizes himself at the point at which he desires to rest, and then neutralizes the Rhythmic swing of the pendulum which would tend to carry him to the other pole. All individuals who have attained any degree of Self-Mastery do this to a certain degree, more or less unconsciously, but the Master does this consciously, and by the use of his Will, and attains a degree of Poise and Mental Firmness almost impossible of belief on the part of the masses who are swung backward and forward like a pendulum. This Principle and that of Polarity have been closely studied by the Hermetists, and the methods of counteracting, neutralizing, and USING them form an important part of the Hermetic Mental Alchemy.

6. The Principle of Cause and Effect

"Every Cause has its Effect; every Effect has its Cause; everything happens according to Law; Chance is but a name for Law not recognized; there are many planes of causation, but nothing escapes the Law."

—THE KYBALION

This Principle embodies the fact that there is a Cause for every Effect; an Effect from every Cause. It explains that: "Everything Happens according to Law"; that nothing ever "merely happens"; that there is no such thing as Chance; that while there are various planes of Cause and Effect, the higher dominating the lower planes, still nothing ever entirely escapes the Law. The Hermetists understand the art and methods of rising above the ordinary plane of Cause and Effect, to a certain degree, and by mentally rising to a higher plane they become Causers instead of Effects. The masses of people are carried along, obedient to environment; the wills and desires of others stronger than themselves; heredity; suggestion; and other outward causes moving them about like pawns on the Chessboard of Life. But the Masters, rising to the plane above, dominate their moods, characters, qualities, and powers, as well as the environment surrounding them, and become Movers instead of pawns. They help to PLAY THE GAME OF LIFE, instead of being played and moved about by other wills and environment. They USE the Principle instead of being its tools. The Masters obey the Causation of the higher planes, but they help to RULE on their own plane. In this statement there is condensed a wealth of Hermetic knowledge—let him read who can.

7. The Principle of Gender

"Gender is in everything; everything has its Masculine and Feminine Principles; Gender manifests on all planes."
—THE KYBALION

This Principle embodies the truth that there is GENDER manifested in everything—the Masculine and Feminine Principles ever at work. This is true not only of the Physical Plane, but of the Mental and even the Spiritual Planes. On the Physical Plane, the Principle manifests as SEX, on the higher planes it takes higher forms, but the Principle is ever the same. No creation, physical, mental or spiritual, is possible without this Principle. An understanding of its laws will throw light on many a subject that has perplexed the minds of men. The Principle of Gender works ever in the direction of generation, regeneration, and creation. Everything, and every person, contains the two Elements or Principles, or this great Principle, within it, him or her. Every Male thing has the Female Element also; every Female contains also the Male Principle. If you would understand the philosophy of Mental and Spiritual Creation, Generation, and Re-generation, you must understand and study this Hermetic Principle. It contains the solution of many mysteries of Life. We caution you that this Principle has no reference to the many base, pernicious and degrading lustful theories, teachings and practices, which are taught under fanciful titles, and which are a prostitution of the great natural principle of Gender. Such base revivals of the ancient infamous forms of Phallicism tend to ruin mind, body and soul, and the Hermetic Philosophy has ever sounded the warning note against these degraded teachings which tend toward lust, licentiousness, and perversion of Nature's principles. If you seek such teachings, you must go elsewhere for them—Hermeticism contains nothing for you along these lines. To the pure, all things are pure; to the base, all things are base.

3

Mental Transmutation

"Mind (as well as metals and elements) may be transmuted, from state to state; degree to degree; condition to condition; pole to pole; vibration to vibration. True Hermetic Transmutation is a Mental Art."

—THE KYBALION

As we have stated, the Hermetists were the original alchemists, astrologers, and psychologists, Hermes having been the founder of these schools of thought. From astrology has grown modern astronomy; from alchemy has grown modern chemistry; from the mystic psychology has grown the modern psychology of the schools. But it must not be supposed that the ancients were ignorant of that which the modern schools suppose to be their exclusive and special property. The records engraved on the stones of Ancient Egypt show conclusively that the ancients had a full comprehensive knowledge of astronomy, the very building of the Pyramids showing the connection between their design and the study of astronomical science. Nor were they ignorant of Chemistry, for the fragments of the ancient writings show that they were acquainted with the chemical properties of things; in fact, the ancient theories regarding physics are being slowly verified by the latest discoveries of modern science, notably those relating to the constitution of matter. Nor must it be supposed that they were ignorant of the so-called modern discoveries in psychology—on the contrary, the Egyptians were especially skilled in the science of Psychology, particularly in the branches that the modern schools ignore, but which, nevertheless, are being uncovered under the name of "psychic science" which is perplexing the psychologists of to-day, and making them reluctantly admit that "there may be something in it after all."

The truth is, that beneath the material chemistry, astronomy and psychology (that is, the psychology in its phase of "brain-action"), the ancients possessed a knowledge of transcendental astronomy, called astrology; of transcendental chemistry, called alchemy; of transcendental psychology, called mystic psychology. They possessed the Inner Knowledge as well as the Outer Knowledge, the latter alone being possessed by modern scientists. Among the many secret branches of knowledge possessed by the Hermetists, was that known as Mental Transmutation, which forms the subject matter of this lesson.

"Transmutation" is a term usually employed to designate the ancient art of the transmutation of metals—particularly of the base metals into gold. The word "Transmute" means "to change from one nature, form, or substance, into another; to transform" (Webster). And accordingly, "Mental Transmutation" means the art of changing and transforming mental states, forms, and conditions, into others. So you may see that Mental Transmutation is the "Art of Mental Chemistry," if you like the term—a form of practical Mystic Psychology.

But this means far more than appears on the surface. Transmutation, Alchemy, or Chemistry, on the Mental Plane is important enough in its effects, to be sure, and if the art stopped there it would still be one of the most important branches of study known to man. But this is only the beginning. Let us see why!

The first of the Seven Hermetic Principles is the Principle of Mentalism, the axiom of which is "THE ALL is Mind; the Universe is Mental," which means that the Underlying Reality of the Universe is Mind; and the Universe itself is Mental—that is, "existing in the Mind of THE ALL." We shall consider this Principle in succeeding lessons, but let us see the effect of the principle if it be assumed to be true.

If the Universal is Mental in its nature, then Mental Transmutation must be the art of CHANGING THE CONDITIONS OF THE UNIVERSE, along the lines of Matter, Force and Mind. So you see, therefore, that Mental Transmutation is really the "Magic" of which the ancient writers had so much to say in their mystical works, and about which they gave so few practical instructions. If All be Mental, then the art which enables one to transmute mental conditions must render the Master the controller of material conditions as well as those ordinarily called "mental."

As a matter of fact, none but advanced Mental Alchemists have been able to attain the degree of power necessary to control the grosser physical conditions, such as the control of the elements of Nature; the production or cessation of tempests; the production and cessation of earthquakes and other great physical phenomena. But that such men have existed, and do exist to-day, is a matter of earnest belief to all advanced occultists of all schools. That the Masters exist, and have these powers, the best teachers assure their students, having had experiences which justify them in such belief and statements. These Masters do not make public exhibitions of their powers, but seek seclusion from the crowds of men, in order to better work their way along the Path of Attainment. We mention their existence, at this point, merely to call your attention to the fact that their power is entirely Mental, and operates along the lines of the higher Mental Transmutation, under the Hermetic Principle of Mentalism. "The Universe is Mental"—*The Kybalion*.

But students and Hermetists of lesser degree than Masters— the Initiates and Teachers—are able to freely work along the Mental Plane, in Mental Transmutation. In fact all that we call "psychic phenomena"; "mental influence"; "mental science"; "new-thought phenomena," etc., operates along the same general lines, for there is but one principle involved, no matter by what name the phenomena be called.

The student and practitioner of Mental Transmutation works among the Mental Plane, transmuting mental conditions, states, etc., into others, according to various formulas, more or less efficacious. The various "treatments," "affirmations," "denials," etc., of the schools of mental science are but formulas, often quite imperfect and unscientific, of The Hermetic Art. The majority of modern practitioners are quite ignorant compared to the ancient masters, for they lack the fundamental knowledge upon which the work is based.

Not only may the mental states, etc., of one's self be changed or transmuted by Hermetic Methods; but also the states of others may be, and are, constantly transmuted in the same way, usually unconsciously, but often consciously by some understanding of the laws and principles, in cases where the people affected are not informed of the principles of self-protection. And more than this, as many students and practitioners of modern mental science know, every material condition depending upon the minds of other people may be changed or transmuted in accordance with the earnest desire, will, and "treatments" of the person desiring changed conditions of life. The public are so generally informed regarding these things at present, that we do not deem it necessary to mention the same at length, our purpose at this point being merely to show the Hermetic Principle and Art underlying all of these various forms of practice, good and evil, for the force can be used in opposite directions according to the Hermetic Principles of Polarity.

In this little book we shall state the basic principles of Mental Transmutation, that all who read may grasp the Underlying Principles, and thus possess the Master-Key that will unlock the many doors of the Principle of Polarity.

We shall now proceed to a consideration of the first of the Hermetic Seven Principles—the Principle of Mentalism, in which is explained the truth that "THE ALL is Mind; the Universe is Mental," in the words of *The Kybalion*. We ask the close attention, and careful study of this great Principle, on the part of our students, for it is really the Basic Principle of the whole Hermetic Philosophy, and of the Hermetic Art of Mental Transmutation.

4

The All

"Under, and back of, the Universe of Time, Space and Change, is ever to be found The Substantial Reality—the Fundamental Truth."

—THE KYBALION

"Substance" means: "that which underlies all outward manifestations; the essence; the essential reality; the thing in itself," etc. "Substantial" means: "actually existing; being the essential element; being real," etc. "Reality" means: "the state of being real; true, enduring; valid; fixed; permanent; actual," etc.

Under and behind all outward appearances or manifestations, there must always be a Substantial Reality. This is the Law. Man considering the Universe, of which he is a unit, sees nothing but change in matter, forces, and mental states. He sees that nothing really IS, but that everything is BECOMING and CHANGING. Nothing stands still—everything is being born, growing, dying—the very instant a thing reaches its height, it begins to decline—the law of rhythm is in constant operation—there is no reality, enduring quality, fixity, or substantiality in anything—nothing is permanent but Change. He sees all things evolving from other things, and resolving into other things—a constant action and reaction; inflow and outflow; building up and tearing down; creation and destruction; birth, growth and death. Nothing endures but Change. And if he be a thinking man, he realizes that all of these changing things must be but outward appearances or manifestations of some Underlying Power—some Substantial Reality.

All thinkers, in all lands and in all times, have assumed the necessity for postulating the existence of this Substantial Reality. All philosophies worthy of the name have been based upon this thought. Men have given to this Substantial Reality many names—some have called it by the term of Deity (under many titles); others have called it "The Infinite and Eternal Energy"; others have tried to call it "Matter"—but all have acknowledged its existence. It is self-evident—it needs no argument.

In these lessons we have followed the example of some of the world's greatest thinkers, both ancient and modern—the Hermetic Masters—and have called this Underlying Power—this Substantial Reality—by the Hermetic name of "THE ALL," which term we consider the most comprehensive of the many terms applied by Man to THAT which transcends names and terms.

We accept and teach the view of the great Hermetic thinkers of all times, as well as of those illumined souls who have reached higher planes of being, both of whom assert that the inner nature of THE ALL is UNKNOWABLE. This must be so, for naught but THE ALL itself can comprehend its own nature and being.

The Hermetists believe and teach that THE ALL, "in itself," is and must ever be UNKNOWABLE. They regard all the theories, guesses and speculations of the theologians and metaphysicians regarding the inner nature of THE ALL, as but the childish efforts of mortal minds to grasp the secret of the Infinite. Such efforts have always failed and will always fail, from the very nature of the task. One pursuing such inquiries travels around and around in the labyrinth of thought, until he is lost to all sane reasoning, action or conduct, and is utterly unfitted for the work of life. He is like the squirrel which frantically runs around and around the circling treadmill wheel of his cage, traveling ever and yet reaching nowhere—at the end a prisoner still, and standing just where he started.

And still more presumptuous are those who attempt to ascribe to THE ALL the personality, qualities, properties, characteristics and attributes of themselves, ascribing to THE ALL the human emotions, feelings, and characteristics, even down to the pettiest qualities of mankind, such as jealousy, susceptibility to flattery and praise, desire for offerings and worship, and all the other survivals from the days of the childhood of the race. Such ideas are not worthy of grown men and women, and are rapidly being discarded.

(At this point, it may be proper for me to state that we make a distinction between Religion and Theology—between Philosophy and Metaphysics. Religion, to us, means that intuitional realization of the existence of THE ALL, and one's relationship to it; while Theology means the attempts of men to ascribe personality, qualities, and characteristics to it; their theories regarding its affairs, will, desires, plans, and designs; and their assumption of the office of "middle-men" between THE ALL and the people. Philosophy, to us, means the inquiry after knowledge of things knowable and thinkable; while Metaphysics means the attempt to carry the inquiry over and beyond the boundaries and into regions unknowable and unthinkable, and with the same tendency as that of Theology. And consequently, both Religion and Philosophy mean to us things having roots in Reality, while Theology and Metaphysics seem like broken reeds, rooted in the quicksands of ignorance, and affording naught but the most insecure support for the mind or soul of Man. We do not insist upon our students accepting these definitions—we mention them merely to show our position. At any rate, you shall hear very little about Theology and Metaphysics in these lessons.)

But while the essential nature of THE ALL is Unknowable, there are certain truths connected with its existence which the human mind finds itself compelled to accept. And an examination of these reports form a proper subject of inquiry, particularly as they agree with the reports of the Illumined on higher planes. And to this inquiry we now invite you.

"THAT which is the Fundamental Truth—the Substantial Reality—is beyond true naming, but the Wise Men call it THE ALL."

—THE KYBALION

"In its Essence, THE ALL is UNKNOWABLE."

—THE KYBALION

"But, the report of Reason must be hospitably received, and treated with respect."

—THE KYBALION

The human reason, whose reports we must accept so long as we think at all, informs us as follows regarding THE ALL, and that without attempting to remove the veil of the Unknowable:

1. THE ALL must be ALL that REALLY IS. There can be nothing existing outside of THE ALL, else THE ALL would not be THE ALL.

2. THE ALL must be INFINITE, for there is nothing else to define, confine, bound, limit or restrict THE ALL. It must be Infinite in Time, or ETERNAL,—it must have always continuously existed, for there is nothing else to have ever created it, and something can never evolve from nothing, and if it had ever "not been," even for a moment, it would not "be" now,—it must continuously exist forever, for there is nothing to destroy it, and it can never "not-be," even for a moment, because something can never become nothing. It must be Infinite in Space—it must be Everywhere, for there is no place outside of THE ALL—it cannot be otherwise than continuous in Space, without break, cessation, separation, or interruption, for there is nothing to break, separate, or interrupt its continuity, and nothing with which to "fill in the gaps." It must be Infinite in Power, or Absolute, for there is nothing to limit, restrict, restrain, confine, disturb or condition it—it is subject to no other Power, for there is no other Power.

3. THE ALL must be IMMUTABLE, or not subject to change in its real nature, for there is nothing to work changes upon it; nothing into which it could change, nor from which it could have changed. It cannot be added to nor subtracted

from; increased nor diminished; nor become greater or lesser in any respect whatsoever. It must have always been, and must always remain, just what it is now—THE ALL—there has never been, is not now, and never will be, anything else into which it can change.

4. THE ALL being Infinite, Absolute, Eternal and Unchangeable it must follow that anything finite, changeable, fleeting, and conditioned cannot be THE ALL. And as there is Nothing outside of THE ALL, in Reality, then any and all such finite things must be as Nothing in Reality. Now do not become befogged, nor frightened—we are not trying to lead you into the Christian Science field under cover of Hermetic Philosophy. There is a Reconciliation of this apparently contradictory state of affairs. Be patient, we will reach it in time.

We see around us that which is called "Matter," which forms the physical foundation for all forms. Is THE ALL merely Matter? Not at all! Matter cannot manifest Life or Mind, and as Life and Mind are manifested in the Universe, THE ALL cannot be Matter, for nothing rises higher than its own source—nothing is ever manifested in an effect that is not in the cause—nothing is evolved as a consequent that is not involved as an antecedent. And then Modern Science informs us that there is really no such thing as Matter—that what we call Matter is merely "interrupted energy or force," that is, energy or force at a low rate of vibration. As a recent writer has said "Matter has melted into Mystery." Even Material Science has abandoned the theory of Matter, and now rests on the basis of "Energy."

Then is THE ALL mere Energy or Force? Not Energy or Force as the materialists use the terms, for their energy and force are blind, mechanical things, devoid of Life or Mind. Life and Mind can never evolve from blind Energy or Force, for the reason given a moment ago: "Nothing can rise higher than its source—nothing is evolved unless it is involved—nothing manifests in the effect, unless it is in the cause." And so THE ALL cannot be mere Energy or Force, for, if it were, then there would be no such things as Life and Mind in existence, and we know better than that, for we are Alive and using Mind to consider this very question, and so are those who claim that Energy or Force is Everything.

What is there then higher than Matter or Energy that we know to be existent in the Universe? LIFE AND MIND! Life and Mind in all their varying degrees of unfoldment! "Then," you ask, "do you mean to tell us that THE ALL is LIFE and MIND?" Yes! and No! is our answer. If you mean Life and Mind as we poor petty mortals know them, we say No! THE ALL is not that! "But what kind of Life and Mind do you mean?" you ask.

The answer is "LIVING MIND, as far above that which mortals know by those words, as Life and Mind are higher than mechanical forces, or matter—INFINITE LIVING MIND as compared to finite Life and Mind." We mean that which the illumined souls mean when they reverently pronounce the word: "SPIRIT!"

"THE ALL" is Infinite Living Mind—the Illumined call it SPIRIT!

5

The Mental Universe

"The Universe is Mental—held in the Mind of THE ALL."
—THE KYBALION

THE ALL is SPIRIT! But what is Spirit? This question cannot be answered, for the reason that its definition is practically that of THE ALL, which cannot be explained or defined. Spirit is simply a name that men give to the highest conception of Infinite Living Mind—it means "the Real Essence"—it means Living Mind, as much superior to Life and Mind as we know them, as the latter are superior to mechanical Energy and Matter. Spirit transcends our understanding, and we use the term merely that we may think or speak of THE ALL. For the purposes of thought and understading, we are justified in thinking of Spirit as Infinite Living Mind, at the same time acknowledging that we cannot fully understand it. We must either do this or stop thinking of the matter at all.

Let us now proceed to a consideration of the nature of the Universe, as a whole and in its parts. What is the Universe? We have seen that there can be nothing outside of THE ALL. Then is the Universe THE ALL? No, this cannot be, because the Universe seems to be made up of MANY, and is constantly changing, and in other ways it does not measure up to the ideas that we are compelled to accept regarding THE ALL, as stated in our last lesson. Then if the Universe be not THE ALL, then it must be Nothing—such is the inevitable conclusion of the mind at first thought. But this will not satisfy the question, for we are sensible of the existence of the Universe. Then if the Universe is neither THE ALL, nor Nothing, what can it be? Let us examine this question.

If the Universe exists at all, or seems to exist, it must proceed in some way from THE ALL—it must be a creation of THE ALL. But as something can never come from nothing, from what could THE ALL have created it? Some philosophers have answered this question by saying that THE ALL created the Universe from ITSELF—that is, from the being and substance of THE ALL. But this will not do, for THE ALL cannot be subtracted from, nor divided, as we have seen, and then again if this be so, would not each particle in the Universe be aware of its being THE ALL—THE ALL could not lose its knowledge of itself, nor actually BECOME an atom, or blind force, or lowly living thing. Some men, indeed, realizing that THE ALL is indeed ALL, and also recognizing that they, the men, existed, have jumped to the conclusion that they and THE ALL were identical, and they have filled the air with shouts of "I AM GOD," to the amusement of the multitude and the sorrow of sages. The claim of the corpuscle that: "I am Man!" would be modest in comparison.

But, what indeed is the Universe, if it be not THE ALL, not yet created by THE ALL having separated itself into fragments? What else can it be—of what else can it be made? This is the great question. Let us examine it carefully. We find here that the "Principle of Correspondence" (see Lesson 1.) comes to our aid here. The old Hermetic axiom, "As above so below," may be pressed into service at this point. Let us endeavor to get a glimpse of the workings on higher planes by examining those on our own. The Principle of Correspondence must apply to this as well as to other problems.

Let us see! On his own plane of being, how does Man create? Well, first, he may create by making something out of outside materials. But this will not do, for there are no materials outside of THE ALL with which it may create. Well, then, secondly, Man pro-creates or reproduces his kind by the process of begetting, which is self-multiplication accomplished by transferring a portion of his substance to his offspring. But this will not do, because THE ALL cannot transfer or subtract a portion of itself, nor can it reproduce or multiply itself—in the first place there would be a taking away, and in the second case a multiplication or addition to THE ALL, both thoughts being an absurdity. Is there no third way in which MAN creates? Yes, there is—he CREATES MENTALLY! And in so doing he uses no outside materials, nor does he reproduce himself, and yet his Spirit pervades the Mental Creation.

Following the Principle of Correspondence, we are justified in considering that THE ALL creates the Universe MENTALLY, in a manner akin to the process whereby Man creates Mental Images. And, here is where the report of Reason tallies precisely with the report of the Illumined, as shown by their teachings and writings. Such are the teachings of the Wise Men. Such was the Teaching of Hermes.

THE ALL can create in no other way except mentally, without either using material (and there is none to use), or else reproducing itself (which is also impossible). There is no escape from this conclusion of the Reason, which, as we have said, agrees with the highest teachings of the Illumined. Just as you, student, may create a Universe of your own in your mentality, so does THE ALL create Universes in its own Mentality. But your Universe is the mental creation of a Finite Mind, whereas that of THE ALL is the creation of an Infinite. The two are similar in kind, but infinitely different in degree. We shall examine more closely into the process of creation and manifestation, as we proceed. But this is the point to fix in your minds at this stage: THE UNIVERSE, AND ALL IT CONTAINS, IS A MENTAL CREATION OF THE ALL. Verily, indeed, ALL IS MIND!

> "THE ALL creates in its Infinite Mind countless Universes, which exist for aeons of Time—and yet, to THE ALL, the creation, development, decline and death of a million Universes is as the time of the twinkling of an eye."
>
> —THE KYBALION

> "The Infinite Mind of THE ALL is the womb of Universes."
>
> —THE KYBALION

The Principle of Gender (see Lesson 1. and other lessons to follow) is manifested on all planes of life, material, mental and spiritual. But, as we have said before, "Gender" does not mean "Sex"—sex is merely a material manifestation of gender. "Gender" means "relating to generation or creation." And wherever anything is generated or created, on any plane, the Principle of

Gender must be manifested. And this is true even in the creation of Universes.

Now do not jump to the conclusion that we are teaching that there is a male and female God, or Creator. That idea is merely a distortion of the ancient teachings on the subject. The true teaching is that THE ALL, in itself, is above Gender, as it is above every other Law, including those of Time and Space. It is the Law, from which the Laws proceed, and it is not subject to them. But when THE ALL manifests on the plane of generation or creation, then it acts according to Law and Principle, for it is moving on a lower plane of Being. And consequently it manifests the Principle of Gender, in its Masculine and Feminine aspects, on the Mental Plane, of course.

This idea may seem startling to some of you who hear it for the first time, but you have all really passively accepted it in your everyday conceptions. You speak of the Fatherhood of God, and the Motherhood of Nature—of God, the Divine Father, and Nature the Universal Mother—and have thus instinctively acknowledged the Principle of Gender in the Universe. Is this not so?

But, the Hermetic teaching does not imply a real duality—THE ALL is ONE—the Two Aspects are merely aspects of manifestation. The teaching is that The Masculine Principle manifested by THE ALL stands, in a way, apart from the actual mental creation of the Universe. It projects its Will toward the Feminine Principle (which may be called "Nature") whereupon the latter begins the actual work of the evolution of the Universe, from simple "centres of activity" on to man, and then on and on still higher, all according to well-established and firmly enforced Laws of Nature. If you prefer the old figures of thought, you may think of the Masculine Principle as GOD, the Father, and of the Feminine Principle as NATURE, the Universal Mother, from whose womb all things have been born. This is more than a mere poetic figure of speech—it is an idea of the actual process of the creation of the Universe. But always remember, that THE ALL is but One, and that in its Infinite Mind the Universe is generated, created and exists.

It may help you to get the proper idea, if you will apply the Law of Correspondence to yourself, and your own mind. You know that the part of You which you call "I," in a sense, stands apart and witnesses the creation of Mental Images in your own mind. The part of your mind in which the mental generation is accomplished may be called the "Me" in distinction from the "I" which stands apart and witnesses and examines the thoughts, ideas and images of the "Me." "As above, so below," remember, and the phenomena of one plane may be employed to solve the riddles of higher or lower planes.

Is it any wonder that You, the child, feel that instinctive reverence for THE ALL, which feeling we call "religion"—that respect, and reverence for THE FATHER MIND? Is it any wonder that, when you consider the works and wonders of Nature, you are overcome with a mighty feeling which has its roots away down in your inmost being? It is the MOTHER MIND that you are pressing close up to, like a babe to the breast.

Do not make the mistake of supposing that the little world you see around you—the Earth, which is a mere grain of dust in the Universe—is the Universe itself. There are millions upon millions of such worlds, and greater. And there are millions of millions of such Universes in existence within the Infinite Mind of THE ALL. And even in our own little solar system there are regions and planes of life far higher than ours, and beings compared to which we earth-bound mortals are as the slimy life-forms that dwell on the ocean's bed when compared to Man. There are beings with powers and attributes higher than Man has ever dreamed of the gods' possessing. And yet these beings were once as you, and still lower—and you will be even as they, and still higher, in time, for such is the Destiny of Man as reported by the Illumined.

And Death is not real, even in the Relative sense—it is but Birth to a new life—and You shall go on, and on, and on, to higher and still higher planes of life, for aeons upon aeons of time. The Universe is your home, and you shall explore its farthest recesses before the end of Time. You are dwelling in the Infinite Mind of THE ALL, and your possibilities and opportunities are infinite, both in time and space. And at the end of the Grand Cycle of Aeons, when THE ALL shall draw back into itself all of its creations—you will go gladly, for you will then be able to know the Whole Truth of being At One with THE ALL. Such is the report of the Illumined—those who have advanced well along The Path.

And, in the meantime, rest calm and serene—you are safe and protected by the Infinite Power of the FATHER-MOTHER MIND.

> "Within the Father-Mother Mind, mortal children are at home."
>
> —THE KYBALION

> "There is not one who is Fatherless, nor Motherless in the Universe."
>
> —THE KYBALION

6

The Divine Paradox

"The half-wise, recognizing the comparative unreality of the Universe, imagine that they may defy its Laws—such are vain and presumptuous fools, and they are broken against the rocks and torn asunder by the elements by reason of their folly. The truly wise, knowing the nature of the Universe, use Law against laws; the higher against the lower; and by the Art of Alchemy transmute that which is undesirable into that which is worthy, and thus triumph. Mastery consists not in abnormal dreams, visions and fantastic imaginings or living, but in using the higher forces against the lower—escaping the pains of the lower planes by vibrating on the higher. Transmutation, not presumptuous denial, is the weapon of the Master."

—THE KYBALION

This is the Paradox of the Universe, resulting from the Principle of Polarity which manifests when THE ALL begins to Create—hearken to it for it points the difference between half-wisdom and wisdom. While to THE INFINITE ALL, the Universe, its Laws, its Powers, its Life, its Phenomena, are as things witnessed in the state of Meditation or Dream; yet to

THE BOOK OF HERMETICA

all that is Finite, the Universe must be treated as Real, and life, and action, and thought, must be based thereupon, accordingly, although with an ever understanding of the Higher Truth. Each according to its own Plane and Laws. Were THE ALL to imagine that the Universe were indeed Reality, then woe to the Universe, for there would be then no escape from lower to higher, divineward—then would the Universe become a fixity and progress would become impossible. And if Man, owing to half-wisdom, acts and lives and thinks of the Universe as merely a dream (akin to his own finite dreams) then indeed does it so become for him, and like a sleep-walker he stumbles ever around and around in a circle, making no progress, and being forced into an awakening at last by his falling bruised and bleeding over the Natural Laws which he ignored. Keep your mind ever on the Star, but let your eyes watch over your footsteps, lest you fall into the mire by reason of your upward gaze. Remember the Divine Paradox, that while the Universe IS NOT, still IT IS. Remember ever the Two Poles of Truth— the Absolute and the Relative. Beware of Half-Truths.

What Hermetists know as "the Law of Paradox" is an aspect of the Principle of Polarity. The Hermetic writings are filled with references to the appearance of the Paradox in the consideration of the problems of Life and Being. The Teachers are constantly warning their students against the error of omitting the "other side" of any question. And their warnings are particularly directed to the problems of the Absolute and the Relative, which perplex all students of philosophy, and which cause so many to think and act contrary to what is generally known as "common sense." And we caution all students to be sure to grasp the Divine Paradox of the Absolute and Relative, lest they become entangled in the mire of the Half-Truth. With this in view this particular lesson has been written. Read it carefully!

The first thought that comes to the thinking man after he realizes the truth that the Universe is a Mental Creation of THE ALL, is that the Universe and all that it contains is a mere illusion; an unreality; against which idea his instincts revolt. But this, like all other great truths, must be considered both from the Absolute and the Relative points of view. From the Absolute viewpoint, of course, the Universe is in the nature of an illusion, a dream, a phantasmagoria, as compared to THE ALL in itself. We recognize this even in our ordinary view, for we speak of the world as "a fleeting show" that comes and goes, is born and dies—for the element of impermanence and change, finiteness and unsubstantiality, must ever be connected with the idea of a created Universe when it is contrasted with the idea of THE ALL, no matter what may be our beliefs concerning the nature of both. Philosopher, metaphysician, scientist and theologian all agree upon this idea, and the thought is found in all forms of philosophical thought and religious conceptions, as well as in the theories of the respective schools of metaphysics and theology.

So, the Hermetic Teachings do not preach the unsubstantiality of the Universe in any stronger terms than those more familiar to you, although their presentation of the subject may seem somewhat more startling. Anything that has a beginning and an ending must be, in a sense, unreal and untrue, and the Universe comes under the rule, in all schools of thought. From the Absolute point of view, there is nothing Real except THE ALL, no matter what terms we may use in thinking of, or discussing the subject. Whether the Universe be created of

Matter, or whether it be a Mental Creation in the Mind of THE ALL—it is unsubstantial, non-enduring, a thing of time, space and change. We want you to realize this fact thoroughly, before you pass judgment on the Hermetic conception of the Mental nature of the Universe. Think over any and all of the other conceptions, and see whether this be not true of them.

But the Absolute point of view shows merely one side of the picture—the other side is the Relative one. Absolute Truth has been defined as "Things as the mind of God knows them," while Relative Truth is "Things as the highest reason of Man understands them." And so while to THE ALL the Universe must be unreal and illusionary, a mere dream or result of meditation—nevertheless, to the finite minds forming a part of that Universe, and viewing it through mortal faculties, the Universe is very real indeed, and must be so considered. In recognizing the Absolute view, we must not make the mistake of ignoring or denying the facts and phenomena of the Universe as they present themselves to our mortal faculties—we are not THE ALL, remember.

To take familiar illustrations, we all recognize the fact that Matter "exists" to our senses—we will fare badly if we do not. And yet, even our finite minds understand the scientific dictum that there is no such thing as Matter from a scientific point of view—that which we call Matter is held to be merely an aggregation of atoms, which atoms themselves are merely a grouping of units of force, called electrons or "ions," vibrating and in constant circular motion. We kick a stone and we feel the impact—it seems to be real, notwithstanding that we know it to be merely what we have stated above. But remember that our foot, which feels the impact by means of our brains, is likewise Matter, so constituted of electrons, and for that matter so are our brains. And, at the best, if it were not by reason of our Mind, we would not know the foot or stone at all.

Then again, the ideal of the artist or sculptor, which he is endeavoring to reproduce in stone or on canvas, seems very real to him. So do the characters in the mind of the author, or dramatist, which he seeks to express so that others may recognize them. And if this be true in the case of our finite minds, what must be the degree of Reality in the Mental Images created in the Mind of the Infinite? Oh, friends, to mortals this Universe of Mentality is very real indeed—it is the only one we can ever know, though we rise from plane to plane, higher and higher in it. To know it otherwise, by actual experience, we must be THE ALL itself. It is true that the higher we rise in the scale—the nearer to "the mind of the Father" we reach—the more apparent becomes the illusory nature of finite things, but not until THE ALL finally withdraws us into itself does the vision actually vanish.

So, we need not dwell upon the feature of illusion. Rather let us, recognizing the real nature of the Universe, seek to understand its mental laws, and endeavor to use them to the best effect in our upward progress through life, as we travel from plane to plane of being. The Laws of the Universe are none the less "Iron Laws" because of the mental nature. All, except THE ALL, are bound by them. What is IN THE INFINITE MIND OF THE ALL is REAL in a degree second only to that Reality itself which is vested in the nature of THE ALL.

So, do not feel insecure or afraid—we are all HELD FIRMLY IN THE INFINITE MIND OF THE ALL, and there is naught to hurt us or for us to fear. There is no Power outside of THE

ALL to affect us. So we may rest calm and secure. There is a world of comfort and security in this realization when once attained. Then "calm and peaceful do we sleep, rocked in the Cradle of the Deep"—resting safely on the bosom of the Ocean of Infinite Mind, which is THE ALL. In THE ALL, indeed, do "we live and move and have our being."

Matter is none the less Matter to us, while we dwell on the plane of Matter, although we know it to be merely an aggregation of "electrons," or particles of Force, vibrating rapidly and gyrating around each other in the formations of atoms; the atoms in turn vibrating and gyrating, forming molecules, which latter in turn form larger masses of Matter. Nor does Matter become less Matter, when we follow the inquiry still further, and learn from the Hermetic Teachings, that the "Force" of which the electrons are but units is merely a manifestation of the Mind of THE ALL, and like all else in the Universe is purely Mental in its nature. While on the Plane of Matter, we must recognize its phenomena—we may control Matter (as all Masters of higher or lesser degree do), but we do so by applying the higher forces. We commit a folly when we attempt to deny the existence of Matter in the relative aspect. We may deny its mastery over us—and rightly so—but we should not attempt to ignore it in its relative aspect, at least so long as we dwell upon its plane.

Nor do the Laws of Nature become less constant or effective, when we know them, likewise, to be merely mental creations. They are in full effect on the various planes. We overcome the lower laws, by applying still higher ones—and in this way only. But we cannot escape Law or rise above it entirely. Nothing but THE ALL can escape Law—and that because THE ALL is LAW itself, from which all Laws emerge. The most advanced

Masters may acquire the powers usually attributed to the gods of men; and there are countless ranks of being, in the great hierarchy of life, whose being and power transcends even that of the highest Masters among men to a degree unthinkable by mortals, but even the highest Master, and the highest Being, must bow to the Law, and be as Nothing in the eye of THE ALL. So that if even these highest Beings, whose powers exceed even those attributed by men to their gods—if even these are bound by and are subservient to Law, then imagine the presumption of mortal man, of our race and grade, when he dares to consider the Laws of Nature as "unreal," visionary and illusory, because he happens to be able to grasp the truth that the Laws are Mental in nature, and simply Mental Creations of THE ALL. Those Laws which THE ALL intends to be governing Laws are not to be defied or argued away. So long as the Universe endures, will they endure—for the Universe exists by virtue of these Laws which form its framework and which hold it together.

The Hermetic Principle of Mentalism, while explaining the true nature of the Universe upon the principle that all is Mental, does not change the scientific conceptions of the Universe, Life, or Evolution. In fact, science merely corroborates the Hermetic Teachings. The latter merely teaches that the nature of the Universe is "Mental," while modern science has taught that it is "Material"; or (of late) that it is "Energy" at the last analysis. The Hermetic Teachings have no fault to find with Herbert Spencer's basic principle which postulates the existence of an "Infinite and Eternal Energy, from which all things proceed." In fact, the Hermetics recognize in Spencer's philosophy the highest outside statement of the workings of the Natural Laws that have ever been promulgated, and they believe Spencer to have been a reincarnation of an ancient philosopher who dwelt in ancient Egypt thousands of years ago, and who later incarnated as Heraclitus, the Grecian philosopher who lived B.C. 500. And they regard his statement of the "Infinite and Eternal Energy" as directly in the line of the Hermetic Teachings, always with the addition of their own doctrine that his "Energy" is the Energy of the Mind of THE ALL. With the Master-Key of the Hermetic Philosophy, the student of Spencer will be able to unlock many doors of the inner philosophical conceptions of the great English philosopher, whose work shows the results of the preparation of his previous incarnations. His teachings regarding Evolution and Rhythm are in almost perfect agreement with the Hermetic Teachings regarding the Principle of Rhythm.

So, the student of Hermetics need not lay aside any of his cherished scientific views regarding the Universe. All he is asked to do is to grasp the underlying principle of "THE ALL is Mind; the Universe is Mental—held in the Mind of THE ALL." He will find that the other six of the Seven Principles will "fit into" his scientific knowledge, and will serve to bring out obscure points and to throw light in dark corners. This is not to be wondered at, when we realize the influence of the Hermetic thought on the early philosophers of Greece, upon whose foundations of thought the theories of modern science largely rest. The acceptance of the First Hermetic Principle (Mentalism) is the only great point of difference between Modern Science and Hermetic students, and Science is gradually moving toward the Hermetic position in its groping in the dark for a way out of the Labyrinth into which it has wandered in its search for Reality.

The purpose of this lesson is to impress upon the minds of our students the fact that, to all intents and purposes, the Universe and its laws, and its phenomena, are just as REAL, so far as Man is concerned, as they would be under the hypotheses of Materialism or Energism. Under any hypothesis the Universe in its outer aspect is changing, ever-flowing, and transitory—and therefore devoid of substantiality and reality. But (note the other pole of the truth) under any of the same hypotheses, we are compelled to ACT AND LIVE as if the fleeting things were real and substantial. With this difference, always, between the various hypotheses—that under the old views Mental Power was ignored as a Natural Force, while under Mentalism it becomes the Greatest Natural Force. And this one difference revolutionizes Life, to those who understand the Principle and its resulting laws and practice.

So, finally, students all, grasp the advantage of Mentalism, and learn to know, use and apply the laws resulting there-from. But do not yield to the temptation which, as *The Kybalion* states, overcomes the half-wise and which causes them to be hypnotized by the apparent unreality of things, the consequence being that they wander about like dream-people dwelling in a world of dreams, ignoring the practical work and life of man, the end being that "they are broken against the rocks and torn asunder by the elements, by reason of their folly." Rather follow the example of the wise, which the same authority states, "use Law against Laws; the higher against the lower; and by the Art of Alchemy transmute that which is undesirable into that which is worthy, and thus triumph." Following the authority, let us avoid the half-wisdom (which is folly) which ignores the truth that: "Mastery consists not in abnormal dreams, visions, and fantastic imaginings or living, but in using the higher forces against the lower—escaping the pains of the lower planes by vibrating on the higher." Remember always, student, that "Transmutation, not presumptuous denial, is the weapon of the Master." The above quotations are from *The Kybalion*, and are worthy of being committed to memory by the student.

We do not live in a world of dreams, but in a Universe which, while relative, is real so far as our lives and actions are concerned. Our business in the Universe is not to deny its existence, but to LIVE, using the Laws to rise from lower to higher—living on, doing the best that we can under the circumstances arising each day, and living, so far as is possible, to our highest ideas and ideals. The true Meaning of Life is not known to men on this plane—if, indeed, to any—but the highest authorities, and our own intuitions, teach us that we will make no mistake in living up to the best that is in us, so far as is possible, and realizing the Universal tendency in the same direction in spite of apparent evidences to the contrary. We are all on The Path—and the road leads upward ever, with frequent resting places.

Read the Message of *The Kybalion*—and follow the example of "the wise"—avoiding the mistake of "the half-wise" who perish by reason of their folly.

7

"The All" in All

"While All is in THE ALL, it is equally true that THE ALL is in All. To him who truly understands this truth hath come great knowledge."

—THE KYBALION

How often have the majority of people heard repeated the statement that their Deity (called by many names) was "All in All," and how little have they suspected the inner occult truth concealed by these carelessly uttered words? The commonly used expression is a survival of the ancient Hermetic Maxim quoted above. As *The Kybalion* says: "To him who truly understands this truth, hath come great knowledge." And, this being so, let us seek this truth, the understanding of which means so much. In this statement of truth—this Hermetic Maxim—is concealed one of the greatest philosophical, scientific and religious truths.

We have given you the Hermetic Teaching regarding the Mental Nature of the Universe—the truth that "the Universe is Mental—held in the Mind of THE ALL." As *The Kybalion* says, in the passage quoted above: "All is in THE ALL." But note also the co-related statement, that: "It is equally true that

THE ALL is in ALL." This apparently contradictory statement is reconcilable under the Law of Paradox. It is, moreover, an exact Hermetic statement of the relations existing between THE ALL and its Mental Universe. We have seen how "All is in THE ALL"—now let us examine the other aspect of the subject.

The Hermetic Teachings are to the effect that THE ALL is Imminent in ("remaining within; inherent; abiding within") its Universe, and in every part, particle, unit, or combination, within the Universe. This statement is usually illustrated by the Teachers by a reference to the Principle of Correspondence. The Teacher instructs the student to form a Mental Image of something, a person, an idea, something having a mental form, the favorite example being that of the author or dramatist forming an idea of his characters; or a painter or sculptor forming an image of an ideal that he wishes to express by his art. In each case, the student will find that while the image has its existence, and being, solely within his own mind, yet he, the student, author, dramatist, painter, or sculptor, is, in a sense, immanent in; remaining within; or abiding within, the mental image also. In other words, the entire virtue, life, spirit, of reality in the mental image is derived from the "immanent mind" of the thinker. Consider this for a moment, until the idea is grasped.

To take a modern example, let us say that Othello, Iago, Hamlet, Lear, Richard III, existed merely in the mind of Shakespeare, at the time of their conception or creation. And yet, Shakespeare also existed within each of these characters, giving them their vitality, spirit, and action. Whose is the "spirit" of the characters that we know as Micawber, Oliver Twist, Uriah Heep—is it Dickens, or have each of these characters a personal spirit, independent of their creator? Have the Venus of Medici, the Sistine Madonna, the Appollo Belvidere, spirits and reality of their own, or do they represent the spiritual and mental power of their creators? The Law of Paradox explains that both propositions are true, viewed from the proper viewpoints. Micawber is both Micawber, and yet Dickens. And, again, while Micawber may be said to be Dickens, yet Dickens is not identical with Micawber. Man, like Micawber, may exclaim: "The Spirit of my Creator is inherent within me—and yet I am not HE!" How different this from the shocking half-truth so vociferously announced by certain of the half-wise, who fill the air with their raucous cries of: "I Am God!" Imagine poor Micawber, or the sneaky Uriah Heep, crying: "I Am Dickens"; or some of the lowly clods in one of Shakespeare's plays, grandiloquently announcing that: "I Am Shakespeare!" THE ALL is in the earth-worm, and yet the earth-worm is far from being THE ALL. And still the wonder remains, that though the earth-worm exists merely as a lowly thing, created and having its being solely within the Mind of THE ALL—yet THE ALL is immanent in the earth-worm, and in the particles that go to make up the earth-worm. Can there be any greater mystery than this of "All in THE ALL; and THE ALL in All?"

The student will, of course, realize that the illustrations given above are necessarily imperfect and inadequate, for they represent the creation of mental images in finite minds, while the Universe is a creation of Infinite Mind—and the difference between the two poles separates them. And yet it is merely a matter of degree—the same Principle is in operation—the Principle of Correspondence manifests in each—"As above, so Below; as Below, so above."

And, in the degree that Man realizes the existence of the

Indwelling Spirit immanent within his being, so will he rise in the spiritual scale of life. This is what spiritual development means—the recognition, realization, and manifestation of the Spirit within us. Try to remember this last definition—that of spiritual development. It contains the Truth of True Religion.

There are many planes of Being—many sub-planes of Life— many degrees of existence in the Universe. And all depend upon the advancement of beings in the scale, of which scale the lowest point is the grossest matter, the highest being separated only by the thinnest division from the SPIRIT of THE ALL. And, upward and onward along this Scale of Life, everything is moving. All are on the Path, whose end is THE ALL. All progress is a Returning Home. All is Upward and Onward, in spite of all seemingly contradictory appearances. Such is the Message of the Illumined.

The Hermetic Teachings concerning the process of the Mental Creation of the Universe, are that at the beginning of the Creative Cycle, THE ALL, in its aspect of "Being," projects its Will toward its aspect of "Becoming," and the process of creation begins. It is taught that the process consists of the lowering of Vibration until a very low degree of vibratory energy is reached, at which point the grossest possible form of Matter is manifested. This process is called the stage of Involution, in which THE ALL becomes "involved," or "wrapped up," in its creation. This process is believed by the Hermetists to have a Correspondence to the mental process of an artist, writer, or inventor, who becomes so wrapped up in his mental creation as to almost forget his own existence and who, for the time being, almost "lives in his creation." If instead of "wrapped" we use the word "rapt," perhaps we will give a better idea of what is meant.

This Involuntary stage of Creation is sometimes called the "Outpouring" of the Divine Energy, just as the Evolutionary state is called the "Indrawing." The extreme pole of the Creative process is considered to be the furthest removed from THE ALL, while the beginning of the Evolutionary stage is regarded as the beginning of the return swing of the pendulum of Rhythm—a "coming home" idea being held in all of the Hermetic Teachings.

The Teachings are that during the "Outpouring," the vibrations become lower and lower until finally the urge ceases, and the return swing begins. But there is this difference, that while in the "Outpouring" the creative forces manifest compactly and as a whole, yet from the beginning of the Evolutionary or "Indrawing" stage, there is manifested the Law of Individualization—that is, the tendency to separate into Units of Force, so that finally that which left THE ALL as unindividualized energy returns to its source as countless highly developed Units of Life, having risen higher and higher in the scale by means of Physical, Mental and Spiritual Evolution.

The ancient Hermetists use the word "Meditation," in describing the process of the mental creation of the Universe in the Mind of THE ALL, the word "Contemplation" also being frequently employed. But the idea intended seems to be that of the employment of the Divine Attention. "Attention" is a word derived from the Latin root, meaning "to reach out; to stretch out," and so the act of Attention is really a mental "reaching out; extension" of mental energy, so that the underlying idea is readily understood when we examine into the real meaning of "Attention."

The Hermetic Teachings regarding the process of Evolution are that, THE ALL, having meditated upon the beginning of the Creation—having thus established the material foundations of the Universe—having thought it into existence—then gradually awakens or rouses from its Meditation and in so doing starts into manifestation the process of Evolution, on the material, mental and spiritual planes, successively and in order. Thus the upward movement begins—and all begins to move Spiritward. Matter becomes less gross; the Units spring into being; the combinations begin to form; Life appears and manifests in higher and higher forms; and Mind becomes more and more in evidence—the vibrations constantly becoming higher. In short, the entire process of Evolution, in all of its phases, begins, and proceeds according to the established Laws of the "Indrawing" process. All of this occupies æons upon æons of Man's time, each æon containing countless millions of years, but yet the Illumined inform us that the entire creation, including Involution and Evolution, of a Universe, is but "as the twinkle of the eye" to THE ALL. At the end of countless cycles of æons of time, THE ALL withdraws its Attention—its Contemplation and Meditation—of the Universe, for the Great Work is finished—and All is withdrawn into THE ALL from which it emerged. But Mystery of Mysteries—the Spirit of each soul is not annihilated, but is infinitely expanded—the Created and the Creator are merged. Such is the report of the Illumined!

The above illustration of the "meditation," and subsequent "awakening from meditation," of THE ALL, is of course but an attempt of the Teachers to describe the Infinite process by a finite example. And, yet: "As Below, so Above." The difference is merely in degree. And just as THE ALL arouses itself from the meditation upon the Universe, so does Man (in time) cease from manifesting upon the Material Plane, and withdraws himself more and more into the Indwelling Spirit, which is indeed "The Divine Ego."

There is one more matter of which we desire to speak in this lesson, and that comes very near to an invasion of the Metaphysical field of speculation, although our purpose is merely to show the futility of such speculation. We allude to the question which inevitably comes to the mind of all thinkers who have ventured to seek the Truth. The question is: "WHY does THE ALL create Universes?" The question may be asked in different forms, but the above is the gist of the inquiry.

Men have striven hard to answer this question, but still there is no answer worthy of the name. Some have imagined that THE ALL had something to gain by it, but this is absurd, for what could THE ALL gain that it did not already possess? Others have sought the answer in the idea that THE ALL "wished something to love"; and others that it created for pleasure, or amusement; or because it "was lonely"; or to manifest its power;—all puerile explanations and ideas, belonging to the childish period of thought.

Others have sought to explain the mystery by assuming that THE ALL found itself "compelled" to create, by reason of its own "internal nature"—its "creative instinct." This idea is in advance of the others, but its weak point lies in the idea of THE ALL being "compelled" by anything, internal or external. If its "internal nature," or "creative instinct," compelled it to do anything, then the "internal nature" or "creative instinct" would be the Absolute, instead of THE ALL, and so accordingly that part of the proposition falls. And, yet, THE ALL does create and manifest, and seems to find some kind of satisfaction in so doing. And it is difficult to escape the conclusion that in some infinite degree it must have what would correspond to an "inner nature," or "creative instinct," in man, with correspondingly infinite Desire and Will. It could not act unless it Willed to Act; and it would not Will to Act, unless it Desired to Act; and it would not Desire to Act unless it obtained some Satisfaction thereby. And all of these things would belong to an "Inner Nature," and might be postulated as existing according to the Law of Correspondence. But, still, we prefer to think of THE ALL as acting entirely FREE from any influence, internal as well as external. That is the problem which lies at the root of difficulty—and the difficulty that lies at the root of the problem.

Strictly speaking, there cannot be said to be any "Reason" whatsoever for THE ALL to act, for a "reason" implies a "cause," and THE ALL is above Cause and Effect, except when it Wills to become a Cause, at which time the Principle is set into motion. So, you see, the matter is Unthinkable, just as THE ALL is Unknowable. Just as we say THE ALL merely "IS"—so we are compelled to say that "THE ALL ACTS BECAUSE IT ACTS." At the last, THE ALL is All Reason in Itself; All Law in Itself; All Action in Itself—and it may be said, truthfully, that THE ALL is Its Own Reason; its own Law; its own Act—or still further, that THE ALL; Its Reason; Its Act; is Law; are ONE, all being names for the same thing. In the opinion of those who are giving you these present lessons, the answer is locked up in the INNER SELF of THE ALL, along with its Secret of Being. The Law of Correspondence, in our opinion, reaches only to that aspect of THE ALL, which may be spoken of as "The Aspect of BECOMING." Back of that Aspect is "The Aspect of BEING," in which all Laws are lost in LAW; all Principles merge into PRINCIPLE—and THE ALL; PRINCIPLE; and BEING; are IDENTICAL, ONE AND THE SAME. Therefore, Metaphysical speculation on this point is futile. We go into the matter here, merely to show that we recognize the question, and also the absurdity of the ordinary answers of metaphysics and theology.

In conclusion, it may be of interest to our students to learn that while some of the ancient, and modern, Hermetic Teachers have rather inclined in the direction of applying the Principle of Correspondence to the question, with the result of the "Inner Nature" conclusion—still the legends have it that HERMES, the Great, when asked this question by his advanced students, answered them by PRESSING HIS LIPS TIGHTLY TOGETHER and saying not a word, indicating that there WAS NO ANSWER. But, then, he may have intended to apply the axiom of his philosophy, that: "The lips of Wisdom are closed, except to the ears of Understanding," believing that even his advanced students did not possess the Understanding which entitled them to the Teaching. At any rate, if Hermes possessed the Secret, he failed to impart it, and so far as the world is concerned THE LIPS OF HERMES ARE CLOSED regarding it. And where the Great Hermes hesitated to speak, what mortal may dare to teach?

But, remember, that whatever be the answer to this problem,

if indeed there be an answer—the truth remains that: "While All is in THE ALL, it is equally true that THE ALL is in All." The Teaching on this point is emphatic. And, we may add the concluding words of the quotation: "To him who truly understands this truth, hath come great knowledge."

8

The Planes of Correspondence

"As above, so below; as below, so above."

—THE KYBALION

The great Second Hermetic Principle embodies the truth that there is a harmony, agreement, and correspondence between the several planes of Manifestation, Life and Being. This truth is a truth because all that is included in the Universe emanates from the same source, and the same laws, principles, and characteristics apply to each unit, or combination of units of activity, as each manifests its own phenomena upon its own plane.

For the purpose of convenience of thought and study, the Hermetic Philosophy considers that the Universe may be divided into three great classes of phenomena, known as the Three Great Planes, namely:

1. The Great Physical Plane
2. The Great Mental Plane
3. The Great Spiritual Plane

These divisions are more or less artificial and arbitrary, for the truth is that all of the three divisions are but ascending degrees of the great scale of Life, the lowest point of which is undifferentiated Matter, and the highest point that of Spirit. And, moreover, the different Planes shade into each other, so that no hard and fast division may be made between the higher phenomena of the Physical and the lower of the Mental; or between the higher of the Mental and the lower of the Physical.

In short, the Three Great Planes may be regarded as three great groups of degrees of Life Manifestation. While the purposes of this little book do not allow us to enter into an extended discussion of, or explanation of, the subject of these different planes, still we think it well to give a general description of the same at this point.

At the beginning we may as well consider the question so often asked by the neophyte, who desires to be informed regarding the meaning of the word "Plane," which term has been very freely used, and very poorly explained, in many recent works upon the subject of occultism. The question is generally about as follows: "Is a Plane a place having dimensions, or is it merely a condition or state?" We answer: "No, not a place, nor ordinary dimension of space; and yet more than a state or condition. It may be considered as a state or condition, and yet the state or condition is a degree of dimension, in a scale subject to measurement." Somewhat paradoxical, is it not? But let us examine the matter. A "dimension," you know, is "a measure in a straight line, relating to measure," etc. The ordinary dimensions of space are length, breadth, and height, or perhaps length, breadth, height, thickness or circumference. But there is another dimension of "created things," or "measure in a straight line," known to occultists, and to scientists as well, although the latter have not as yet applied the term "dimension" to it—and this new dimension, which, by the way, is the much speculated-about "Fourth Dimension," is the standard used in determining the degrees or "planes."

This Fourth Dimension may be called "the Dimension of Vibration." It is a fact well known to modern science, as well as to the Hermetists who have embodied the truth in their "Third Hermetic Principle," that "everything is in motion; everything vibrates; nothing is at rest." From the highest manifestation, to the lowest, everything and all things Vibrate. Not only do they vibrate at different rates of motion, but as in different directions and in a different manner. The degrees of the "rate" of vibrations constitute the degrees of measurement on the Scale of Vibrations—in other words the degrees of the Fourth Dimension. And these degrees form what occultists call "Planes." The higher the degree of rate of vibration, the higher the plane, and the higher the manifestation of Life occupying that plane. So that while a plane is not "a place," nor yet "a state or condition," yet it possesses qualities common to both. We shall have more to say regarding the subject of the scale of Vibrations in our next lessons, in which we shall consider the Hermetic Principle of Vibration.

You will kindly remember, however, that the Three Great Planes are not actual divisions of the phenomena of the Universe, but merely arbitrary terms used by the Hermetists in order to aid in the thought and study of the various degrees and forms of universal activity and life. The atom of matter, the unit of force, the mind of man, and the being of the arch-angel are all but degrees in one scale, and all fundamentally the same, the difference between solely a matter of degree, and rate of vibration—all are creations of THE ALL, and have their existence solely within the Infinite Mind of THE ALL.

The Hermetists sub-divide each of the Three Great Planes into Seven Minor Planes, and each of these latter are also subdivided into seven sub-planes, all divisions being more or less arbitrary, shading into each other, and adopted merely for convenience of scientific study and thought.

The Great Physical Plane, and its Seven Minor Planes, is that division of the phenomena of the Universe which includes all that relates to physics, or material things, forces, and manifestations. It includes all forms of that which we call Matter, and all forms of that which we call Energy or Force. But you must remember that the Hermetic Philosophy does not recognize Matter as a "thing in itself," or as having a separate existence even in the Mind of THE ALL. The Teachings are that Matter is but a form of Energy—that is, Energy at a low rate of vibrations of a certain kind. And accordingly the Hermetists classify Matter under the head of Energy, and give to it three of the Seven Minor Planes of the Great Physical Plane.

These Seven Minor Physical Planes are as follows:

1. The Plane of Matter (A)
2. The Plane of Matter (B)
3. The Plane of Matter (C)
4. The Plane of Ethereal Substance
5. The Plane of Energy (A)
6. The Plane of Energy (B)
7. The Plane of Energy (C)

The Plane of Matter (A) comprises the forms of Matter in its form of solids, liquids, and gases, as generally recognized by the text-books on physics. The Plane of Matter (B) comprises certain higher and more subtle forms of Matter of the existence of which modern science is but now recognizing, the phenomena of Radiant Matter, in its phases of radium, etc., belonging to the lower sub-division of this Minor Plane. The Plane of Matter (C) comprises forms of the most subtle and tenuous Matter, the existence of which is not suspected by ordinary scientists. The Plane of Ethereal Substance comprises that which science speaks of as "The Ether," a substance of extreme tenuity and elasticity, pervading all Universal Space, and acting as a medium for the transmission of waves of energy, such as light, heat, electricity, etc. This Ethereal Substance forms a connecting link between Matter (so-called) and Energy, and partakes of the nature of each. The Hermetic Teachings, however, instruct that this plane has seven sub-divisions (as have all of the Minor Planes), and that in fact there are seven ethers, instead of but one.

Next above the Plane of Ethereal Substance comes the Plane of Energy (A), which comprises the ordinary forms of Energy known to science, its seven sub-planes being, respectively, Heat; Light; Magnetism; Electricity; and Attraction (including Gravitation, Cohesion, Chemical Affinity, etc.) and several other forms of energy indicated by scientific experiments but not as yet named or classified. The Plane of Energy (B) comprises seven sub-planes of higher forms of energy not as yet discovered by science, but which have been called "Nature's Finer Forces" and which are called into operation in manifestations of certain forms of mental phenomena, and by which such phenomena becomes possible. The Plane of Energy (C) comprises seven sub-planes of energy so highly organized that it bears many of the characteristics of "life," but which is not recognized by the minds of men on the ordinary plane of development, being available for the use on beings of the Spiritual Plane alone—such energy is unthinkable to ordinary man, and may be considered almost as "the divine power." The beings employing the same are as "gods" compared even to the highest human types known to us.

The Great Mental Plane comprises those forms of "living things" known to us in ordinary life, as well as certain other forms not so well known except to the occultist. The classification of the Seven Minor Mental Planes is more or less satisfactory and arbitrary (unless accompanied by elaborate explanations which are foreign to the purpose of this particular work), but we may as well mention them. They are as follows:

1.   The Plane of Mineral Mind
2.   The Plane of Elemental Mind (A)
3.   The Plane of Plant Mind
4.   The Plane of Elemental Mind (B)
5.   The Plane of Animal Mind
6.   The Plane of Elemental Mind (C)
7.   The Plane of Human Mind

The Plane of Mineral Mind comprises the "states or conditions" of the units or entities, or groups and combinations of the same, which animate the forms known to us as "minerals, chemicals, etc." These entities must not be confounded with the molecules, atoms and corpuscles themselves, the latter being merely the material bodies or forms of these entities, just as a man's body is but his material form and not "himself." These entities may be called "souls" in one sense, and are living beings of a low degree of development, life, and mind—just a little more than the units of "living energy" which comprise the higher sub-divisions of the highest Physical Plane. The average mind does not generally attribute the possession of mind, soul, or life, to the Mineral kingdom, but all occultists recognize the existence of the same, and modern science is rapidly moving forward to the point-of-view of the Hermetic, in this respect. The molecules, atoms and corpuscles have their "loves and hates"; likes and dislikes; "attractions and repulsions"; "affinities and non-affinities," etc., and some of the more daring of modern scientific minds have expressed the opinion that the desire and will, emotions and feelings, of the atoms differ only in degree from those of men. We have no time or space to argue this matter here. All occultists know it to be a fact, and others are referred to some of the more recent scientific works for outside corroboration. There are the usual seven sub-divisions to this plane.

The Plane of Elemental Mind (A) comprises the state or condition, and degree of mental and vital development of a class of entities unknown to the average man, but recognized to occultists. They are invisible to the ordinary senses of man, but, nevertheless, exist and play their part of the Drama of the Universe. Their degree of intelligence is between that of the mineral and chemical entities on the one hand, and of the entities of the plant kingdom on the other. There are seven sub-divisions to this plane, also.

The Plane of Plant Mind, in its seven sub-divisions, comprises the states or conditions of the entities comprising the

THE BOOK OF HERMETICA

kingdoms of the Plant World, the vital and mental phenomena of which is fairly well understood by the average intelligent person, many new and interesting scientific works regarding "Mind and Life in Plants" having been published during the last decade. Plants have life, mind and "souls," as well as have the animals, man, and super-man.

The Plane of Elemental Mind (B), in its seven sub-divisions, comprises the states and conditions of a higher form of "elemental" or unseen entities, playing their part in the general work of the Universe, the mind and life of which form a part of the scale between the Plane of Plant Mind and the Plane of Animal Mind, the entities partaking of the nature of both.

The Plane of Animal Mind, in its seven sub-divisions, comprises the states and conditions of the entities, beings, or souls, animating the animal forms of life, familiar to us all. It is not necessary to go into details regarding this kingdom or plane of life, for the animal world is as familiar to us as is our own.

The Plane of Elemental Mind (C), in its seven sub-divisions, comprises those entities or beings, invisible as are all such elemental forms, which partake of the nature of both animal and human life in a degree and in certain combinations. The highest forms are semi-human in intelligence.

The Plane of Human Mind, in its seven sub-divisions, comprises those manifestations of life and mentality which are common to Man, in his various grades, degrees, and divisions. In this connection, we wish to point out the fact that the average man of to-day occupies but the fourth sub-division of the Plane of Human Mind, and only the most intelligent have crossed the borders of the Fifth Sub-Division. It has taken the race millions of years to reach this stage, and it will take many more years for the race to move on to the sixth and seventh sub-divisions, and beyond. But, remember, that there have been races before us which have passed through these degrees, and then on to higher planes. Our own race is the fifth (with stragglers from the fourth) which has set foot upon The Path. And, then there are a few advanced souls of our own race who have outstripped the masses, and who have passed on to the sixth and seventh sub-division, and some few being still further on. The man of the Sixth Sub-Division will be "The Super-Man"; he of the Seventh will be "The Over-Man."

In our consideration of the Seven Minor Mental Planes, we have merely referred to the Three Elementary Planes in a general way. We do not wish to go into this subject in detail in this work, for it does not belong to this part of the general philosophy and teachings. But we may say this much, in order to give you a little clearer idea of the relations of these planes to the more familiar ones—the Elementary Planes bear the same relation to the Planes of Mineral, Plant, Animal and Human Mentality and Life, that the black keys on the piano do to the white keys. The white keys are sufficient to produce music, but there are certain scales, melodies, and harmonies, in which the black keys play their part, and in which their presence is necessary. They are also necessary as "connecting links" of soul-condition; entity states, etc., between the several other planes, certain forms of development being attained therein—this last fact giving to the reader who can "read between the lines" a new light upon the processes of Evolution, and a new key to the secret door of the "leaps of life" between kingdom and kingdom. The great kingdoms of Elementals are fully recognized by all occultists, and the esoteric writings are full of mention of them. The readers of

THE BOOK OF HERMETICA

Bulwer's "Zanoni" and similar tales will recognize the entities inhabiting these planes of life.

Passing on from the Great Mental Plane to the Great Spiritual Plane, what shall we say? How can we explain these higher states of Being, Life and Mind, to minds as yet unable to grasp and understand the higher sub-divisions of the Plane of Human Mind? The task is impossible. We can speak only in the most general terms. How may Light be described to a man born blind—how sugar, to a man who has never tasted anything sweet—how harmony, to one born deaf?

All that we can say is that the Seven Minor Planes of the Great Spiritual Plane (each Minor Plane having its seven sub-divisions) comprise Beings possessing Life, Mind and Form as far above that of Man of to-day as the latter is above the earthworm, mineral or even certain forms of Energy or Matter. The Life of these Beings so far transcends ours, that we cannot even think of the details of the same; their Minds so far transcend ours, that to them we scarcely seem to "think," and our mental processes seem almost akin to material processes; the Matter of which their forms are composed is of the highest Planes of Matter, nay, some are even said to be "clothed in Pure Energy." What may be said of such Beings?

On the Seven Minor Planes of the Great Spiritual Plane exist Beings of whom we may speak as Angels; Archangels; Demi-Gods. On the lower Minor Planes dwell those great souls whom we call Masters and Adepts. Above them come the Great Hierarchies of the Angelic Hosts, unthinkable to man; and above those come those who may without irreverence be called "The Gods," so high in the scale of Being are they, their being, intelligence and power being akin to those attributed by the races of men to their conceptions of Deity. These Beings are beyond even the highest flights of the human imagination, the word "Divine" being the only one applicable to them. Many of these Beings, as well as the Angelic Host, take the greatest interest in the affairs of the Universe and play an important part in its affairs. These Unseen Divinities and Angelic Helpers extend their influence freely and powerfully, in the process of Evolution, and Cosmic Progress. Their occasional intervention and assistance in human affairs have led to the many legends, beliefs, religions and traditions of the race, past and present. They have superimposed their knowledge and power upon the world, again and again, all under the Law of THE ALL, of course.

But, yet, even the highest of these advanced Beings exist merely as creations of, and in, the Mind of THE ALL, and are subject to the Cosmic Processes and Universal Laws. They are still Mortal. We may call them "gods" if we like, but still they are but the Elder Brethren of the Race—the advanced souls who have outstripped their brethren, and who have foregone the ecstacy of Absorption by THE ALL, in order to help the race on its upward journey along The Path. But, they belong to the Universe, and are subject to its conditions—they are mortal—and their plane is below that of Absolute Spirit.

Only the most advanced Hermetists are able to grasp the Inner Teachings regarding the state of existence, and the powers manifested on the Spiritual Planes. The phenomena is so much higher than that of the Mental Planes that a confusion of ideas would surely result from an attempt to describe the same. Only those whose minds have been carefully trained along the lines of the Hermetic Philosophy for years—yes, those who have brought with them from other incarnations the knowledge acquired

THE BOOK OF HERMETICA

previously—can comprehend just what is meant by the Teaching regarding these Spiritual Planes. And much of these Inner Teachings is held by the Hermetists as being too sacred, important and even dangerous for general public dissemination. The intelligent student may recognize what we mean by this when we state that the meaning of "Spirit" as used by the Hermetists is akin to "Living Power"; "Animated Force"; "Inner Essence"; "Essence of Life," etc., which meaning must not be confounded with that usually and commonly employed in connection with the term, i.e., "religious; ecclesiastical; spirituelle; ethereal; holy," etc., etc. To occultists the word "Spirit" is used in the sense of "The Animating Principle," carrying with it the idea of Power, Living Energy, Mystic Force, etc. And occultists know that that which is known to them as "Spiritual Power" may be employed for evil as well as good ends (in accordance with the Principle of Polarity), a fact which has been recognized by the majority of religions in their conceptions of Satan, Beelzebub, the Devil, Lucifer, Fallen Angels, etc. And so the knowledge regarding these Planes has been kept in the Holy of Holies in all Esoteric Fraternities and Occult Orders—in the Secret Chamber of the Temple. But this may be said here, that those who have attained high spiritual powers and have misused them, have a terrible fate in store for them, and the swing of the pendulum of Rhythm will inevitably swing them back to the furthest extreme of Material existence, from which point they must retrace their steps Spiritward, along the weary rounds of The Path, but always with the added torture of having always with them a lingering memory of the heights from which they fell owing to their evil actions. The legends of the Fallen Angels have a basis in actual facts, as all advanced occultists know. The striving for selfish power on the Spiritual

Planes inevitably results in the selfish soul losing its spiritual balance and falling back as far as it had previously risen. But to even such a soul, the opportunity of a return is given—and such souls make the return journey, paying the terrible penalty according to the invariable Law.

In conclusion we would again remind you that according to the Principle of Correspondence, which embodies the truth: "As Above so Below; as Below, so Above," all of the Seven Hermetic Principles are in full operation on all of the many planes, Physical, Mental and Spiritual. The Principle of Mental Substance of course applies to all the planes, for all are held in the Mind of THE ALL. The Principle of Correspondence manifests in all, for there is a correspondence, harmony and agreement between the several planes. The Principle of Vibration manifests on all planes, in fact the very differences that go to make the "planes" arise from Vibration, as we have explained. The Principle of Polarity manifests on each plane, the extremes of the Poles being apparently opposite and contradictory. The Principle of Rhythm manifests on each Plane, the movement of the phenomena having its ebb and flow, rise and flow, incoming and outgoing. The Principle of Cause and Effect manifests on each Plane, every Effect having its Cause and every Cause having its effect. The Principle of Gender manifests on each Plane, the Creative Energy being always manifest, and operating along the lines of its Masculine and Feminine Aspects.

"As Above so Below; as Below, so Above." This centuries old Hermetic axiom embodies one of the great Principles of Universal Phenomena. As we proceed with our consideration of the remaining Principles, we will see even more clearly the truth of the universal nature of this great Principle of Correspondence.

9

Vibration

"Nothing rests; everything moves; everything vibrates."

—THE KYBALION

The great Third Hermetic Principle—the Principle of Vibration—embodies the truth that Motion is manifest in everything in the Universe—that nothing is at rest—that everything moves, vibrates, and circles. This Hermetic Principle was recognized by some of the early Greek philosophers who embodied it in their systems. But, then, for centuries it was lost sight of by the thinkers outside of the Hermetic ranks. But in the Nineteenth Century physical science re-discovered the truth and the Twentieth Century scientific discoveries have added additional proof of the correctness and truth of this centuries-old Hermetic doctrine.

The Hermetic Teachings are that not only is everything in constant movement and vibration, but that the "differences" between the various manifestations of the universal power are due entirely to the varying rate and mode of vibrations. Not only this, but that even THE ALL, in itself, manifests a constant vibration of such an infinite degree of intensity and rapid motion that it may be practically considered as at rest, the teachers directing the attention of the students to the fact that even on the physical plane a rapidly moving object (such as a revolving wheel) seems to be at rest. The Teachings are to the effect that Spirit is at one end of the Pole of Vibration, the other Pole being certain extremely gross forms of Matter. Between these two poles are millions upon millions of different rates and modes of vibration.

Modern Science has proven that all that we call Matter and Energy are but "modes of vibratory motion," and some of the more advanced scientists are rapidly moving toward the positions of the occultists who hold that the phenomena of Mind are likewise modes of vibration or motion. Let us see what science has to say regarding the question of vibrations in matter and energy.

In the first place, science teaches that all matter manifests, in some degree, the vibrations arising from temperature or heat. Be an object cold or hot—both being but degrees of the same things—it manifests certain heat vibrations, and in that sense is in motion and vibration. Then all particles of Matter are in circular movement, from corpuscle to suns. The planets revolve around suns, and many of them turn on their axes. The suns move around greater central points, and these are believed to move around still greater, and so on, ad infinitum. The molecules of which the particular kinds of Matter are composed are in a state of constant vibration and movement around each other and against each other. The molecules are composed of Atoms, which, likewise, are in a state of constant movement and vibration. The atoms are composed of Corpuscles, sometimes called "electrons," "ions," etc., which also are in a state of rapid motion, revolving around each other, and which manifest a very rapid state and mode of vibration. And, so we see that all forms of Matter manifest Vibration, in accordance with the Hermetic Principle of Vibration.

And so it is with the various forms of Energy. Science teaches that Light, Heat, Magnetism and Electricity are but forms of vibratory motion connected in some way with, and probably emanating from the Ether. Science does not as yet attempt to explain the nature of the phenomena known as Cohesion, which is the principle of Molecular Attraction; nor Chemical Affinity, which is the principle of Atomic Attraction; nor Gravitation (the greatest mystery of the three), which is the principle of attraction by which every particle or mass of Matter is bound to every other particle or mass. These three forms of Energy are not as yet understood by science, yet the writers incline to the opinion that these too are manifestations of some form of vibratory energy, a fact which the Hermetists have held and taught for ages past.

The Universal Ether, which is postulated by science without its nature being understood clearly, is held by the Hermetists to be but a higher manifestation of that which is erroneously called matter—that is to say, Matter at a higher degree of vibration—and is called by them "The Ethereal Substance." The Hermetists teach that this Ethereal Substance is of extreme tenuity and elasticity, and pervades universal space, serving as a medium of transmission of waves of vibratory energy, such as heat, light, electricity, magnetism, etc. The Teachings are that The Ethereal Substance is a connecting link between the forms of vibratory energy known as "Matter" on the one hand, and "Energy or Force" on the other; and also that it manifests a degree of vibration, in rate and mode, entirely its own.

Scientists have offered the illustration of a rapidly moving wheel, top, or cylinder, to show the effects of increasing rates of vibration. The illustration supposes a wheel, top, or revolving cylinder, running at a low rate of speed—we will call this revolving thing "the object" in following out the illustration. Let us suppose the object moving slowly. It may be seen readily, but no sound of its movement reaches the ear. The speed is gradually increased. In a few moments its movement becomes so rapid that a deep growl or low note may be heard. Then as the rate is increased the note rises one in the musical scale. Then, the motion being still further increased, the next highest note is distinguished. Then, one after another, all the notes of the musical scale appear, rising higher and higher as the motion is increased. Finally when the motions have reached a certain rate the final note perceptible to human ears is reached and the shrill, piercing shriek dies away, and silence follows. No sound is heard from the revolving object, the rate of motion being so high that the human ear cannot register the vibrations. Then comes the perception of rising degrees of Heat. Then after quite a time the eye catches a glimpse of the object becoming a dull dark reddish color. As the rate increases, the red becomes brighter. Then as the speed is increased, the red melts into an orange. Then the orange melts into a yellow. Then follow, successively, the shades of green, blue, indigo, and finally violet, as the rate of speed increases. Then the violet shades away, and all color disappears, the human eye not being able to register them. But there are invisible rays emanating from the revolving object, the rays that are used in photographing, and other subtle rays of light. Then begin to manifest the peculiar rays known as the "X Rays," etc., as the constitution of the object changes.

Electricity and Magnetism are emitted when the appropriate rate of vibration is attained.

When the object reaches a certain rate of vibration its molecules disintegrate, and resolve themselves into the original elements or atoms. Then the atoms, following the Principle of Vibration, are separated into the countless corpuscles of which they are composed. And finally, even the corpuscles disappear and the object may be said to be composed of The Ethereal Substance. Science does not dare to follow the illustration further, but the Hermetists teach that if the vibrations be continually increased the object would mount up the successive states of manifestation and would in turn manifest the various mental stages, and then on Spiritward, until it would finally re-enter THE ALL, which is Absolute Spirit. The "object," however, would have ceased to be an "object" long before the stage of Ethereal Substance was reached, but otherwise the illustration is correct inasmuch as it shows the effect of constantly increased rates and modes of vibration. It must be remembered, in the above illustration, that at the stages at which the "object" throws off vibrations of light, heat, etc., it is not actually "resolved" into those forms of energy (which are much higher in the scale), but simply that it reaches a degree of vibration in which those forms of energy are liberated, in a degree, from the confining influences of its molecules, atoms and corpuscles, as the case may be. These forms of energy, although much higher in the scale than matter, are imprisoned and confined in the material combinations, by reason of the energies manifesting through, and using material forms, but thus becoming entangled and confined in their creations of material forms, which, to an extent, is true of all creations, the creating force becoming involved in its creation.

But the Hermetic Teachings go much further than do those of modern science. They teach that all manifestation of thought, emotion, reason, will or desire, or any mental state or condition, are accompanied by vibrations, a portion of which are thrown off and which tend to affect the minds of other persons by "induction." This is the principle which produces the phenomena of "telepathy"; mental influence, and other forms of the action and power of mind over mind, with which the general public is rapidly becoming acquainted, owing to the wide dissemination of occult knowledge by the various schools, cults and teachers along these lines at this time.

Every thought, emotion or mental state has its corresponding rate and mode of vibration. And by an effort of the will of the person, or of other persons, these mental states may be reproduced, just as a musical tone may be reproduced by causing an instrument to vibrate at a certain rate—just as color may be reproduced in the same way. By a knowledge of the Principle of Vibration, as applied to Mental Phenomena, one may polarize his mind at any degree he wishes, thus gaining a perfect control over his mental states, moods, etc. In the same way he may affect the minds of others, producing the desired mental states in them. In short, he may be able to produce on the Mental Plane that which science produces on the Physical Plane—namely, "Vibrations at Will." This power of course may be acquired only by the proper instruction, exercises, practice, etc., the science being that of Mental Transmutation, one of the branches of the Hermetic Art.

A little reflection on what we have said will show the student that the Principle of Vibration underlies the wonderful phenomena of the power manifested by the Masters and Adepts, who are able to apparently set aside the Laws of Nature, but who, in reality, are simply using one law against another; one principle against others; and who accomplish their results by changing the vibrations of material objects, or forms of energy, and thus perform what are commonly called "miracles."

As one of the old Hermetic writers has truly said: "He who understands the Princible of Vibration, has grasped the sceptre of Power."

10

Polarity

"Everything is dual; everything has poles; everything has its pair of opposites; like and unlike are the same; opposites are identical in nature, but different in degree; extremes meet; all truths are but half-truths; all paradoxes may be reconciled."

—THE KYBALION

The great Fourth Hermetic Principle—the Principle of Polarity—embodies the truth that all manifested things have "two sides"; "two aspects"; "two poles"; a "pair of opposites," with manifold degrees between the two extremes. The old paradoxes, which have ever perplexed the mind of men, are explained by an understanding of this Principle. Man has always recognized something akin to this Principle, and has endeavored to express it by such sayings, maxims and aphorisms as the following: "Everything is and isn't, at the same time"; "all truths are but half-truths"; "every truth is half-false"; "there are two sides to everything"; "there is a reverse side to every shield," etc., etc.

The Hermetic Teachings are to the effect that the difference between things seemingly diametrically opposed to each other is merely a matter of degree. It teaches that "the pairs of opposites may be reconciled," and that "thesis and anti-thesis are identical in nature, but different in degree"; and that the "universal reconciliation of opposites" is effected by a recognition of this Principle of Polarity. The teachers claim that illustrations of this Principle may be had on every hand, and from an examination into the real nature of anything. They begin by showing that Spirit and Matter are but the two poles of the same thing, the intermediate planes being merely degrees of vibration. They show that THE ALL and The Many are the same, the difference being merely a matter of degree of Mental Manifestation. Thus the LAW and Laws are the two opposite poles of one thing. Likewise, PRINCIPLE and Principles. Infinite Mind and finite minds.

Then passing on to the Physical Plane, they illustrate the Principle by showing that Heat and Cold are identical in nature, the differences being merely a matter of degrees. The thermometer shows many degrees of temperature, the lowest pole being called "cold," and the highest "heat." Between these two poles are many degrees of "heat" or "cold," call them either and you are equally correct. The higher of two degrees is always "warmer," while the lower is always "colder." There is no absolute standard—all is a matter of degree. There is no place on the thermometer where heat ceases and cold begins. It is all a matter of higher or lower vibrations. The very terms "high" and "low," which we are compelled to use, are but poles of the same thing—the terms are relative. So with "East and West"—travel around the world in an eastward direction, and you reach a point which is called west at your starting point, and you return from that westward point. Travel far enough North, and you will find yourself traveling South, or vice versa.

Light and Darkness are poles of the same thing, with many degrees between them. The musical scale is the same—starting with "C" you move upward until you reach another "C," and so on, the differences between the two ends of the board being the same, with many degrees between the two extremes. The scale of color is the same—higher and lower vibrations being the only difference between high violet and low red. Large and Small are relative. So are Noise and Quiet; Hard and Soft follow the rule. Likewise Sharp and Dull. Positive and Negative are two poles of the same thing, with countless degrees between them.

Good and Bad are not absolute—we call one end of the scale Good and the other Bad, or one end Good and the other Evil, according to the use of the terms. A thing is "less good" than the thing higher in the scale; but that "less good" thing, in turn, is "more good" than the thing next below it—and so on, the "more or less" being regulated by the position on the scale.

And so it is on the Mental Plane. "Love and Hate" are generally regarded as being things diametrically opposed to each other; entirely different; unreconcilable. But we apply the Principle of Polarity; we find that there is no such thing as Absolute Love or Absolute Hate, as distinguished from each other. The two are merely terms applied to the two poles of the same thing. Beginning at any point of the scale we find "more love," or "less hate," as we ascend the scale; and "more hate" or "less love" as we descend—this being true no matter from what point, high or low, we may start. There are degrees of Love and Hate, and there is a middle point where "Like and Dislike" become so faint that it is difficult to distinguish between them. Courage and Fear come under the same rule. The Pairs of Opposites exist everywhere. Where you find one thing you find its opposite—the two poles.

And it is this fact that enables the Hermetist to transmute one mental state into another, along the lines of Polarization. Things belonging to different classes cannot be transmuted into each other, but things of the same class may be changed, that is, may have their polarity changed. Thus Love never becomes East or West, or Red or Violet—but it may and often does turn into Hate—and likewise Hate may be transformed into Love, by changing its polarity. Courage may be transmuted into Fear, and the reverse. Hard things may be rendered Soft. Dull things become Sharp. Hot things become Cold. And so on, the transmutation always being between things of the same kind of different degrees. Take the case of a Fearful man. By raising his mental vibrations along the line of Fear-Courage, he can be filled with the highest degree of Courage and Fearlessness. And, likewise, the Slothful man may change himself into an Active, Energetic individual, simply by polarizing along the lines of the desired quality.

The student who is familiar with the processes by which the various schools of Mental Science, etc., produce changes in the mental states of those following their teachings, may not readily understand the principle underlying many of these changes. When, however, the Principle of Polarity is once grasped, and it is seen that the mental changes are occasioned by a change of polarity—a sliding along the same scale—the matter is more readily understood. The change is not in the nature of a transmutation of one thing into another thing entirely different—but is merely a change of degree in the same things, a vastly important difference. For instance, borrowing an analogy from the Physical Plane, it is impossible to change Heat into Sharpness, Loudness, Highness, etc., but Heat may readily be transmuted into Cold, simply by lowering the vibrations. In the same way Hate and Love are mutually transmutable; so are Fear and Courage. But Fear cannot be transformed into Love, nor can Courage be transmuted into Hate. The mental states belong to innumerable classes, each class of which has its opposite poles, along which transmutation is possible.

The student will readily recognize that in the mental states, as well as in the phenomena of the Physical Plane, the two poles may be classified as Positive and Negative, respectively. Thus Love is Positive to Hate; Courage to Fear; Activity to Non-Activity, etc., etc. And it will also be noticed that even to those unfamiliar with the Principle of Vibration, the Positive pole seems to be of a higher degree than the Negative, and readily dominates it. The tendency of Nature is in the direction of the dominant activity of the Positive pole.

In addition to the changing of the poles of one's own mental states by the operation of the art of Polarization, the phenomena of Mental Influence, in its manifold phases, shows us that the principle may be extended so as to embrace the phenomena of the influence of one mind over that of another, of which so much has been written and taught of late years. When it is understood that Mental Induction is possible, that is that mental states may be produced by "induction" from others, then we can readily see how a certain rate of vibration, or polarization of a certain mental state, may be communicated to another person, and his polarity in that class of mental states thus changed.

It is along this principle that the results of many of the "mental treatments" are obtained. For instance, a person is "blue," melancholy and full of fear. A mental scientist bringing his own mind up to the desired vibration by his trained will, and thus obtaining the desired polarization in his own case, then produces a similar mental state in the other by induction, the result being that the vibrations are raised and the person polarizes toward the Positive end of the scale instead of toward the Negative, and his Fear and other negative emotions are transmuted to Courage and similar positive mental states. A little study will show you that these mental changes are nearly all along the line of Polarization, the change being one of degree rather than of kind.

A knowledge of the existence of this great Hermetic Principle will enable the student to better understand his own mental states, and those of other people. He will see that these states are all matters of degree, and seeing thus, he will be able to raise or lower the vibration at will—to change his mental poles, and thus be Master of his mental states, instead of being their servant and slave. And by his knowledge he will be able to aid his fellows intelligently, and by the appropriate methods change the polarity when the same is desirable. We advise all students to familiarize themselves with this Principle of Polarity, for a correct understanding of the same will throw light on many difficult subjects.

11

Rhythm

"Everything flows out and in; everything has its tides; all things rise and fall; the pendulum-swing manifests in everything; the measure of the swing to the right, is the measure of the swing to the left; rhythm compensates."

—THE KYBALION

The great Fifth Hermetic Principle—the Principle of Rhythm—embodies the truth that in everything there is manifested a measured motion; a to-and-from movement; a flow and inflow; a swing forward and backward; a pendulum-like movement; a tide-like ebb and flow; a high-tide and a low-tide; between the two-poles manifest on the physical, mental or spiritual planes. The Principle of Rhythm is closely connected with the Principle of Polarity described in the preceding chapter. Rhythm manifests between the two poles established by the Principle of Polarity. This does not mean, however, that the pendulum of Rhythm swings to the extreme poles, for this rarely happens; in fact, it is difficult to establish the extreme polar opposites in the majority of cases. But the swing is ever "toward" first one pole and then the other.

There is always an action and reaction; an advance and a retreat; a rising and a sinking; manifested in all of the airs and phenomena of the Universe. Suns, worlds, men, animals, plants, minerals, forces, energy, mind and matter, yes, even Spirit, manifests this Principle. The Principle manifests in the creation and destruction of worlds; in the rise and fall of nations; in the life history of all things; and finally in the mental states of Man.

Beginning with the manifestations of Spirit—of THE ALL—it will be noticed that there is ever the Outpouring and the Indrawing; the "Outbreathing and Inbreathing of Brahm," as the Brahmans word it. Universes are created; reach their extreme low point of materiality; and then begin their upward swing. Suns spring into being, and then their height of power being reached, the process of retrogression begins, and after æons they become dead masses of matter, awaiting another impulse which starts again their inner energies into activity and a new solar life cycle is begun. And thus it is with all the worlds; they are born, grow and die; only to be reborn. And thus it is with all the things of shape and form; they swing from action to reaction; from birth to death; from activity to inactivity—and then back again. Thus it is with all living things; they are born, grow, and die—and then are reborn. So it is with all great movements, philosophies, creeds, fashions, governments, nations, and all else—birth, growth, maturity, decadence, death—and then new-birth. The swing of the pendulum is ever in evidence.

Night follows day; and day night. The pendulum swings from Summer to Winter, and then back again. The corpuscles, atoms, molecules, and all masses of matter, swing around the circle of their nature. There is no such thing as absolute rest, or cessation from movement, and all movement partakes of Rhythm. The principle is of universal application. It may be applied to any question, or phenomena of any of the many planes of life. It may be applied to all phases of human activity. There is always the Rhythmic swing from one pole to the other. The Universal Pendulum is ever in motion. The Tides of Life flow in and out, according to Law.

The Principle of Rhythm is well understood by modern science, and is considered a universal law as applied to material things. But the Hermetists carry the principle much further, and know that its manifestations and influence extend to the mental activities of Man, and that it accounts for the bewildering succession of moods, feelings and other annoying and perplexing changes that we notice in ourselves. But the Hermetists by studying the operations of this Principle have learned to escape some of its activities by Transmutation.

The Hermetic Masters long since discovered that while the Principle of Rhythm was invariable, and ever in evidence in mental phenomena, still there were two planes of its manifestation so far as mental phenomena are concerned. They discovered that there were two general planes of Consciousness, the Lower and the Higher, the understanding of which fact enabled them to rise to the higher plane and thus escape the swing of the Rhythmic pendulum which manifested on the lower plane. In other words, the swing of the pendulum occurred on the Unconscious Plane, and the Consciousness was not affected. This they call the Law of Neutralization. Its operations consist in the raising of the Ego above the vibrations of the Unconscious Plane of mental activity, so that the negative-swing of the pendulum is not manifested in consciousness, and therefore they are not affected. It is akin to rising above a thing and letting it pass beneath you. The Hermetic Master, or advanced student, polarizes himself at the desired pole, and by a process akin to "refusing" to participate in the backward swing, or, if you prefer, a "denial" of its influence over him, he stands firm in his polarized position, and allows the mental pendulum to swing back along the unconscious plane. All individuals who have attained any degree of self-mastery, accomplish this, more or less unknowingly, and by refusing to allow their moods and negative mental states to affect them, they apply the Law of Neutralization. The Master, however, carries this to a much higher degree of proficiency, and by the use of his Will he attains a degree of Poise and Mental Firmness almost impossible of belief on the part of those who allow themselves to be swung backward and forward by the mental pendulum of moods and feelings.

The importance of this will be appreciated by any thinking person who realizes what creatures of moods, feelings and emotion the majority of people are, and how little mastery of themselves they manifest. If you will stop and consider a moment, you will realize how much these swings of Rhythm have affected you in your life—how a period of Enthusiasm has been invariably followed by an opposite feeling and mood of Depression. Likewise, your moods and periods of Courage have been succeeded by equal moods of Fear. And so it has ever been with the majority of persons—tides of feeling have ever risen and fallen with them, but they have never suspected the cause or reason of the mental phenomena. An understanding of the workings of this Principle will give one the key to the Mastery of these rhythmic swings of feeling, and will enable him to know himself better and to avoid being carried away by these inflows and outflows. The Will is superior to the conscious manifestation of this Principle, although the Principle itself can never be destroyed. We may escape its effects, but the Principle operates, nevertheless. The pendulum ever swings, although we may escape being carried along with it.

There are other features of the operation of this Principle of Rhythm of which we wish to speak at this point. There comes into its operations that which is known as the Law of Compensation. One of the definitions or meanings of the word "Compensate" is, "to counterbalance," which is the sense in which the Hermetists use the term. It is this Law of Compensation to which *The Kybalion* refers when it says: "The measure of the swing to the right is the measure of the swing to the left; rhythm compensates."

The Law of Compensation is that the swing in one direction determines the swing in the opposite direction, or to the opposite pole—the one balances, or counterbalances, the other. On the Physical Plane we see many examples of this Law. The pendulum of the clock swings a certain distance to the right, and then an equal distance to the left. The seasons balance each other in the same way. The tides follow the same Law. And the same Law is manifested in all the phenomena of Rhythm. The pendulum, with a short swing in one direction, has but a short swing in the other; while the long swing to the right invariably means the long swing to the left. An object hurled upward to a certain height has an equal distance to traverse on its return. The force with which a projectile is sent upward a mile is reproduced when the projectile returns to the earth on its return journey. This Law is constant on the Physical Plane, as reference to the standard authorities will show you.

But the Hermetists carry it still further. They teach that a man's mental states are subject to the same Law. The man who enjoys keenly, is subject to keen suffering; while he who feels but little pain is capable of feeling but little joy. The pig suffers but little mentally, and enjoys but little—he is compensated. And on the other hand, there are other animals who enjoy keenly, but whose nervous organism and temperament cause them to suffer exquisite degrees of pain. And so it is with Man. There are temperaments which permit of but low degrees of enjoyment, and equally low degrees of suffering; while there are others which permit the most intense enjoyment, but also the most intense suffering. The rule is that the capacity for pain and pleasure, in each individual, are balanced. The Law of Compensation is in full operation here.

But the Hermetists go still further in this matter. They teach that before one is able to enjoy a certain degree of pleasure, he must have swung as far, proportionately, toward the other pole of feeling. They hold, however, that the Negative is precedent to the Positive in this matter, that is to say that in experiencing a certain degree of pleasure it does not follow that he will have to "pay up for it" with a corresponding degree of pain; on the contrary, the pleasure is the Rhythmic swing, according to the Law of Compensation, for a degree of pain previously experienced either in the present life, or in a previous incarnation. This throws a new light on the Problem of Pain.

The Hermetists regard the chain of lives as continuous, and as forming a part of one life of the individual, so that in consequence the rhythmic swing is understood in this way, while it would be without meaning unless the truth of reincarnation is admitted.

But the Hermetists claim that the Master or advanced student is able, to a great degree, to escape the swing toward Pain, by the process of Neutralization before mentioned. By rising on to the higher plane of the Ego, much of the experience that comes to those dwelling on the lower plane is avoided and escaped.

The Law of Compensation plays an important part in the lives of men and women. It will be noticed that one generally "pays the price" of anything he possesses or lacks. If he has one thing, he lacks another—the balance is struck. No one can "keep his penny and have the bit of cake" at the same time. Everything has its pleasant and unpleasant sides. The things that one gains are always paid for by the things that one loses. The rich possess much that the poor lack, while the poor often possess things that are beyond the reach of the rich. The millionaire may have the inclination toward feasting, and the wealth wherewith to secure all the dainties and luxuries of the table, while he lacks the appetite to enjoy the same; he envies the appetite and digestion of the laborer, who lacks the wealth and inclinations of the millionaire, and who gets more pleasure from his plain food than the millionaire could obtain even if his appetite were not jaded, nor his digestion ruined, for the wants, habits and inclinations differ. And so it is through life. The Law of Compensation is ever in operation, striving to balance and counter-balance, and always succeeding in time, even though several lives may be required for the return swing of the Pendulum of Rhythm.

12

Causation

"Every Cause has its Effect; every Effect has its Cause; everything happens according to Law; Chance is but a name for Law not recognized; there are many planes of causation, but nothing escapes the Law."

—THE KYBALION

The great Sixth Hermetic Principle—the Principle of Cause and Effect—embodies the truth that Law pervades the Universe; that nothing happens by Chance; that Chance is merely a term indicating cause existing but not recognized or perceived; that phenomena is continuous, without break or exception.

The Principle of Cause and Effect underlies all scientific thought, ancient and modern, and was enunciated by the Hermetic Teachers in the earliest days. While many and varied disputes between the many schools of thought have since arisen, these disputes have been principally upon the details of the operations of the Principle, and still more often upon the meaning of certain words. The underlying Principle of Cause and Effect has been accepted as correct by practically all the thinkers of the world worthy of the name. To think otherwise would be to take the phenomena of the universe from the domain of Law and Order, and to relegate it to the control of the imaginary something which men have called "Chance."

A little consideration will show anyone that there is in reality no such thing as pure Chance. Webster defines the word "Chance" as follows: "A supposed agent or mode of activity other than a force, law or purpose; the operation or activity of such agent; the supposed effect of such an agent; a happening; fortuity; casualty, etc." But a little consideration will show you that there can be no such agent as "Chance," in the sense of something outside of Law—something outside of Cause and Effect. How could there be a something acting in the phenomenal universe, independent of the laws, order, and continuity of the latter? Such a something would be entirely independent of the orderly trend of the universe, and therefore superior to it. We can imagine nothing outside of THE ALL being outside of the Law, and that only because THE ALL is the LAW in itself. There is no room in the universe for a something outside of and independent of Law. The existence of such a Something would render all Natural Laws ineffective, and would plunge the universe into chaotic disorder and lawlessness.

A careful examination will show that what we call "Chance" is merely an expression relating to obscure causes; causes that we cannot perceive; causes that we cannot understand. The word Chance is derived from a word meaning "to fall" (as the falling of dice), the idea being that the fall of the dice (and many other happenings) are merely a "happening" unrelated to any cause. And this is the sense in which the term is generally employed. But when the matter is closely examined, it is seen that there is no chance whatsoever about the fall of the dice. Each time a die falls, and displays a certain number, it obeys a law as infallible as that which governs the revolution of the planets around the sun. Back of the fall of the die are causes, or chains of causes, running back further than the mind can follow. The position of the die in the box; the amount of muscular energy expended in the throw; the condition of the table, etc., etc., all are causes, the effect of which may be seen. But back of these seen causes there are chains of unseen preceding causes, all of which had a bearing upon the number of the die which fell uppermost.

If a die be cast a great number of times, it will be found that the numbers shown will be about equal, that is, there will be an equal number of one-spot, two-spot, etc., coming uppermost. Toss a penny in the air, and it may come down either "heads" or "tails"; but make a sufficient number of tosses, and the heads and tails will about even up. This is the operation of the law of average. But both the average and the single toss come under the Law of Cause and Effect, and if we were able to examine into the preceding causes, it would be clearly seen that it was simply impossible for the die to fall other than it did, under the same circumstances and at the same time. Given the same causes, the same results will follow. There is always a "cause" and a "because" to every event. Nothing ever "happens" without a cause, or rather a chain of causes.

Some confusion has arisen in the minds of persons considering this Principle, from the fact that they were unable to explain how one thing could cause another thing—that is, be the "creator" of the second thing. As a matter of fact, no "thing" ever causes or "creates" another "thing." Cause and Effect deals merely with "events." An "event" is "that which comes, arrives or happens, as a result or consequent of some preceding event."

No event "creates" another event, but is merely a preceding link in the great orderly chain of events flowing from the creative energy of THE ALL. There is a continuity between all events precedent, consequent and subsequent. There is a relation existing between everything that has gone before, and everything that follows. A stone is dislodged from a mountain side and crashes through a roof of a cottage in the valley below. At first sight we regard this as a chance effect, but when we examine the matter we find a great chain of causes behind it. In the first place there was the rain which softened the earth supporting the stone and which allowed it to fall; then back of that was the influence of the sun, other rains, etc., which gradually disintegrated the piece of rock from a larger piece; then there were the causes which led to the formation of the mountain, and its upheaval by convulsions of nature, and so on ad infinitum. Then we might follow up the causes behind the rain, etc. Then we might consider the existence of the roof. In short, we would soon find ourselves involved in a mesh of cause and effect, from which we would soon strive to extricate ourselves.

Just as a man has two parents, and four grandparents, and eight great-grandparents, and sixteen great-great-grandparents, and so on until when, say, forty generations are calculated the numbers of ancestors run into many millions—so it is with the number of causes behind even the most trifling event or phenomena, such as the passage of a tiny speck of soot before your eye. It is not an easy matter to trace the bit of soot back to the early period of the world's history when it formed a part of a massive tree-trunk, which was afterward converted into coal, and so on, until as the speck of soot it now passes before your vision on its way to other adventures. And a mighty chain of events, causes and effects, brought it to its present condition, and the latter is but one of the chain of events which will go to produce other events hundreds of years from now. One of the series of events arising from the tiny bit of soot was the writing of these lines, which caused the typesetter to perform certain work; the proofreader to do likewise; and which will arouse certain thoughts in your mind, and that of others, which in turn will affect others, and so on, and on, and on, beyond the ability of man to think further—and all from the passage of a tiny bit of soot, all of which shows the relativity and association of things, and the further fact that "there is no great; there is no small; in the mind that causeth all."

Stop to think a moment. If a certain man had not met a certain maid, away back in the dim period of the Stone Age— you who are now reading these lines would not now be here. And if, perhaps, the same couple had failed to meet, we who now write these lines would not now be here. And the very act of writing, on our part, and the act of reading, on yours, will affect not only the respective lives of yourself and ourselves, but will also have a direct, or indirect, affect upon many other people now living and who will live in the ages to come. Every thought we think, every act we perform, has its direct and in-direct results which fit into the great chain of Cause and Effect.

We do not wish to enter into a consideration of Free-Will, or Determinism, in this work, for various reasons. Among the many reasons, is the principal one that neither side of the controversy is entirely right—in fact, both sides are partially right, according to the Hermetic Teachings. The Principle of Polarity shows that both are but Half-Truths—the opposing poles of Truth. The Teachings are that a man may be both Free and yet bound by Necessity, depending upon the meaning of the terms, and the height of Truth from which the matter is examined. The ancient writers express the matter thus: "The further the creation is from the Centre, the more it is bound; the nearer the Centre it reaches, the nearer Free is it."

The majority of people are more or less the slaves of heredity, environment, etc., and manifest very little Freedom. They are swayed by the opinions, customs and thoughts of the outside world, and also by their emotions, feelings, moods, etc. They manifest no Mastery, worthy of the name. They indignantly repudiate this assertion, saying, "Why, I certainly am free to act and do as I please—I do just what I want to do," but they fail to explain whence arise the "want to" and "as I please." What makes them "want to" do one thing in preference to another; what makes them "please" to do this, and not do that? Is there no "because" to their "pleasing" and "wanting"? The Master can change these "pleases" and "wants" into others at the opposite end of the mental pole. He is able to "Will to will," instead of to will because some feeling, mood, emotion, or environmental suggestion arouses a tendency or desire within him so to do.

The majority of people are carried along like the falling stone, obedient to environment, outside influences and internal moods, desires, etc., not to speak of the desires and wills of others stronger than themselves, heredity, environment, and suggestion, carrying them along without resistence on their part, or the exercise of the Will. Moved like the pawns on the checkerboard of life, they play their parts and are laid aside after the game is over. But the Masters, knowing the rules of the game, rise above the plane of material life, and placing themselves in touch with the higher powers of their nature, dominate their own moods, characters, qualities, and polarity, as well as the environment surrounding them and thus become Movers in the game, instead of Pawns—Causes instead of Effects. The Masters do not escape the Causation of the higher planes, but fall in with the higher laws, and thus master circumstances on the lower plane. They thus form a conscious part of the Law, instead of being mere blind instruments. While they Serve on the Higher Planes, they Rule on the Material Plane.

But, on higher and on lower, the Law is always in operation. There is no such things as Chance. The blind goddess has been abolished by Reason. We are able to see now, with eyes made clear by knowledge, that everything is governed by Universal Law—that the infinite number of laws are but manifestations of the One Great Law—the LAW which is THE ALL. It is true indeed that not a sparrow drops unnoticed by the Mind of THE ALL—that even the hairs on our head are numbered—as the scriptures have said. There is nothing outside of Law; nothing that happens contrary to it. And yet, do not make the mistake of supposing that Man is but a blind automaton—far from that. The Hermetic Teachings are that Man may use Law to overcome laws, and that the higher will always prevail against the lower, until at last he has reached the stage in which he seeks refuge in the LAW itself, and laughs the phenomenal laws to scorn. Are you able to grasp the inner meaning of this?

13

Gender

"Gender is in everything; everything has its Masculine and Feminine Principles; Gender manifests on all planes."
—THE KYBALION

The great Seventh Hermetic Principle—the Principle of Gender—embodies the truth that there is Gender manifested in everything—that the Masculine and Feminine principles are ever present and active in all phases of phenomena, on each and every plane of life. At this point we think it well to call your attention to the fact that Gender, in its Hermetic sense, and Sex in the ordinarily accepted use of the term, are not the same.

The word "Gender" is derived from the Latin root meaning "to beget; to procreate; to generate; to create; to produce." A moment's consideration will show you that the word has a much broader and more general meaning than the term "Sex," the latter referring to the physical distinctions between male and female living things. Sex is merely a manifestation of Gender on a certain plane of the Great Physical Plane—the plane of organic life. We wish to impress this distinction upon your minds, for the reason that certain writers, who have acquired a smattering of the Hermetic Philosophy, have sought to identify this Seventh Hermetic Principle with wild and fanciful, and often reprehensible, theories and teachings regarding Sex.

The office of Gender is solely that of creating, producing, generating, etc., and its manifestations are visible on every plane of phenomena. It is somewhat difficult to produce proofs of this along scientific lines, for the reason that science has not as yet recognized this Principle as of universal application. But still some proofs are forthcoming from scientific sources. In the first place, we find a distinct manifestation of the Principle of Gender among the corpuscles, ions, or electrons, which constitute the basis of Matter as science now knows the latter, and which by forming certain combinations form the Atom, which until lately was regarded as final and indivisible.

The latest word of science is that the atom is composed of a multitude of corpuscles, electrons, or ions (the various names being applied by different authorities) revolving around each other and vibrating at a high degree and intensity. But the accompanying statement is made that the formation of the atom is really due to the clustering of negative corpuscles around a positive one—the positive corpuscles seeming to exert a certain influence upon the negative corpuscles, causing the latter to assume certain combinations and thus "create" or "generate" an atom. This is in line with the most ancient Hermetic Teachings, which have always identified the Masculine principle of Gender with the "Positive," and the Feminine with the "Negative" Poles of Electricity (so-called).

Now a word at this point regarding this identification. The public mind has formed an entirely erroneous impression regarding the qualities of the so-called "Negative" pole of electrified or magnetized Matter. The terms Positive and Negative are very wrongly applied to this phenomennon by science. The word Positive means something real and strong, as compared with a Negative unreality or weakness. Nothing is further from the real facts of electrical phenomena. The so-called Negative pole of the battery is really the pole in and by which the generation or production of new forms and energies is manifested. There is nothing "negative" about it. The best scientific authorities now use the word "Cathode" in place of "Negative," the word Cathode coming from the Greek root meaning "descent; the path of generation, etc." From the Cathode pole emerge the swarm of electrons or corpuscles; from the same pole emerge those wonderful "rays" which have revolutionized scientific conceptions during the past decade. The Cathode pole is the Mother of all of the strange phenomena which have rendered useless the old text-books, and which have caused many long accepted theories to be relegated to the scrap-pile of scientific speculation. The Cathode, or Negative Pole, is the Mother Principle of Electrical Phenomena, and of the finest forms of matter as yet known to science. So you see we are justified in refusing to use the term "Negative" in our consideration of the subject, and in insisting upon substituting the word "Feminine" for the old term. The facts of the case bear us out in this, without taking the Hermetic Teachings into consideration. And so we shall use the word "Feminine" in the place of "Negative" in speaking of that pole of activity.

The latest scientific teachings are that the creative corpuscles or electrons are Feminine (science says "they are composed of negative electricity"—we say they are composed of Feminine energy). A Feminine corpuscle becomes detached from, or rather leaves, a Masculine corpuscle, and starts on a new career. It actively seeks a union with a Masculine corpuscle, being urged thereto by the natural impulse to create new forms of Matter or Energy. One writer goes so far as to use the term "it at once seeks, of its own volition, a union," etc. This detachment and uniting form the basis of the greater part of the activities of the chemical world. When the Feminine corpuscle unites with a Masculine corpuscle, a certain process is begun. The Feminine particles vibrate rapidly under the influence of the Masculine energy, and circle rapidly around the latter. The result is the birth of a new atom. This new atom is really composed of a union of the Masculine and Feminine electrons, or corpuscles, but when the union is formed the atom is a separate thing, having certain properties, but no longer manifesting the property of free electricity. The process of detachment or separation of the Feminine electrons is called "ionization." These electrons, or corpuscles, are the most active workers in Nature's field. Arising from their unions, or combinations, manifest the varied phenomena of light, heat, electricity, magnetism, attraction, repulsion, chemical affinity and the reverse, and similar phenomena. And all this arises from the operation of the Principle of Gender on the plane of Energy.

The part of the Masculine principle seems to be that of directing a certain inherent energy toward the Feminine principle, and thus starting into activity the creative processes. But the Feminine principle is the one always doing the active creative work—and this is so on all planes. And yet, each principle is incapable of operative energy without the assistance of the other. In some of the forms of life, the two principles are combined in one organism. For that matter, everything in the organic world manifests both genders—there is always the Masculine present in the Feminine form, and the Feminine form. The Hermetic Teachings include much regarding the operation of the two principles of Gender in the production and manifestation of various forms of energy, etc., but we do not deem it expedient to go into detail regarding the same at this point, because we are unable to back up the same with scientific proof, for the reason that science has not as yet progressed thus far. But the example we have given you of the phenomena of the electrons or corpuscles will show you that science is on the right path, and will also give you a general idea of the underlying principles.

Some leading scientific investigators have announced their belief that in the formation of crystals there was to be found something that corresponded to "sex-activity," which is another straw showing the direction the scientific winds are blowing. And each year will bring other facts to corroborate the correctness of the Hermetic Principle of Gender. It will be found that Gender is in constant operation and manifestation in the field of inorganic matter, and in the field of Energy or Force. Electricity is now generally regarded as the "Something" into which all other forms of energy seem to melt or dissolve. The "Electrical Theory of the Universe" is the latest scientific doctrine, and is growing rapidly in popularity and general acceptance. And it thus follows that if we are able to discover in the phenomena of electricity—even at the very root and source of its manifestations—a clear and unmistakable evidence of the presence of Gender and its activities, we are justified in asking you to believe that science at last has offered proofs of the existence in all universal phenomena of that great Hermetic Principle—the Principle of Gender.

THE BOOK OF HERMETICA

It is not necessary to take up your time with the well known phenomena of the "attraction and repulsion" of the atoms; chemical affinity; the "loves and hates" of the atomic particles; the attraction or cohesion between the molecules of matter. These facts are too well known to need extended comment from us. But, have you ever considered that all of these things are manifestations of the Gender Principle? Can you not see that the phenomena is "on all fours" with that of the corpuscles or electrons? And more than this, can you not see the reasonableness of the Hermetic Teachings which assert that the very Law of Gravitation—that strange attraction by reason of which all particles and bodies of matter in the universe tend toward each other—is but another manifestation of the Principle of Gender, which operates in the direction of attracting the Masculine to the Feminine energies, and vice versa? We cannot offer you scientific proof of this at this time—but examine the phenomena in the light of the Hermetic Teachings on the subject, and see if you have not a better working hypothesis than any offered by physical science. Submit all physical phenomena to the test, and you will discern the Principle of Gender ever in evidence.

Let us now pass on to a consideration of the operation of the Principle on the Mental Plane. Many interesting features are there awaiting examination.

14

Mental Gender

Students of psychology who have followed the modern trend of thought along the lines of mental phenomena are struck by the persistence of the dual-mind idea which has manifested itself so strongly during the past ten or fifteen years, and which has given rise to a number of plausible theories regarding the nature and constitution of these "two minds." The late Thomson J. Hudson attained great popularity in 1893 by advancing his well-known theory of the "objective and subjective minds" which he held existed in every individual. Other writers have attracted almost equal attention by the theories regarding the "conscious and sub-conscious minds"; the "voluntary and involuntary minds"; "the active and passive minds," etc., etc. The theories of the various writers differ from each other, but there remains the underlying principle of "the duality of mind."

The student of the Hermetic Philosophy is tempted to smile when he reads and hears of these many "new theories" regarding the duality of mind, each school adhering tenaciously to its own pet theories, and each claiming to have "discovered the truth." The student turns back the pages of occult history, and away back in the dim beginnings of occult teachings he finds references to the ancient Hermetic doctrine of the Principle of Gender on the Mental Plane—the manifestation of Mental Gender. And examining further he finds that the ancient philosophy took cognizance of the phenomenon of the "dual mind," and accounted for it by the theory of Mental Gender. This idea of Mental Gender may be explained in a few words to students who are familiar with the modern theories just alluded to. The Masculine Principle of Mind corresponds to the so-called Objective Mind; Conscious Mind; Voluntary Mind; Active Mind, etc. And the Feminine Principle of Mind corresponds to the so-called Subjective Mind; Sub-conscious Mind; Involuntary Mind; Passive Mind, etc. Of course the Hermetic Teachings do not agree with the many modern theories regarding the nature of the two phases of mind, nor does it admit many of the facts claimed for the two respective aspects—some of the said theories and claims being very far-fetched and incapable of standing the test of experiment and demonstration. We point to the phases of agreement merely for the purpose of helping the student to assimilate his previously acquired knowledge with the teachings of the Hermetic Philosophy. Students of Hudson will notice the statement at the beginning of his second chapter of "The Law of Psychic Phenomena," that: "The mystic jargon of the Hermetic philosophers discloses the same general idea"— i.e., the duality of mind. If Dr. Hudson had taken the time and trouble to decipher a little of "the mystic jargon of the Hermetic Philosophy," he might have received much light upon the subject of "the dual mind"—but then, perhaps, his most interesting work might not have been written. Let us now consider the Hermetic Teachings regarding Mental Gender.

The Hermetic Teachers impart their instruction regarding this subject by bidding their students examine the report of their consciousness regarding their Self. The students are bidden to turn their attention inward upon the Self dwelling within each. Each student is led to see that his consciousness gives him first a report of the existence of his Self—the report is "I Am." This at first seems to be the final words from the consciousness, but a little further examination discloses the fact that this "I Am" may be separated or split into two distinct parts, or aspects, which while working in unison and in conjunction, yet, nevertheless, may be separated in consciousness.

While at first there seems to be only an "I" existing, a more careful and closer examination reveals the fact that there exists an "I" and a "Me." These mental twins differ in their characteristics and nature, and an examination of their nature and the phenomena arising from the same will throw much light upon many of the problems of mental influence.

Let us begin with a consideration of the "Me," which is usually mistaken for the "I" by the student, until he presses the inquiry a little further back into the recesses of consciousness. A man thinks of his Self (in its aspect of "Me") as being composed of certain feelings, tastes, likes, dislikes, habits, peculiar ties, characteristics, etc., all of which go to make up his personality, or the "Self" known to himself and others. He knows that these emotions and feelings change; are born and die away; are subject to the Principle of Rhythm, and the Principle of Polarity, which take him from one extreme of feeling to another. He also thinks of the "Me" as being certain knowledge gathered together in his mind, and thus forming a part of himself. This is the "Me" of a man.

But we have proceeded too hastily. The "Me" of many men may be said to consist largely of their consciousness of the body and their physical appetites, etc. Their consciousness being largely bound up with their bodily nature, they practically "live there." Some men even go so far as to regard their personal apparel as a part of their "Me," and actually seem to consider it a part of themselves. A writer has humorously said that "men consist of three parts—soul, body and clothes." These "clothes conscious" people would lose their personality if divested of their clothing by savages upon the occasion of a shipwreck. But even many who are not so closely bound up with the idea of personal raiment stick closely to the consciousness of their bodies being their "Me." They cannot conceive of a Self independent of the body. Their mind seems to them to be practically "a something belonging to" their body—which in many cases it is indeed.

But as man rises in the scale of consciousness he is able to disentangle his "Me" from his idea of body, and is able to think of his body as "belonging to" the mental part of him. But even then he is very apt to identify the "Me" entirely with the mental states, feelings, etc., which he feels to exist within him. He is very apt to consider these internal states as identical with himself, instead of there being simply "things" produced by some part of his mentality, and existing within him—of him, and in him, but still not "himself." He sees that he may change these internal states of feelings by an effort of will, and that he may produce a feeling or state of an exactly opposite nature, in the same way, and yet the same "Me" exists. And so after a while he is able to set aside these various mental states, emotions, feelings, habits, qualities, characteristics, and other personal mental belongings—he is able to set them aside in the "not-me" collection of curiosities and encumbrances, as well as valuable possessions. This requires much mental concentration and power of mental analysis on the part of the student. But still the task is possible for the advanced student, and even those not so far advanced are able to see, in the imagination, how the process may be performed.

After this laying-aside process has been performed, the student will find himself in conscious possession of a "Self" which may be considered in its "I" and "Me" dual aspects. The "Me" will be felt to be a Something mental in which thoughts, ideas, emotions, feelings, and other mental states may be produced. It may be considered as the "mental womb," as the ancients styled it—capable of generating mental offspring. It reports to the consciousness as a "Me" with latent powers of creation and generation of mental progeny of all sorts and kinds. Its powers of creative energy are felt to be enormous. But still it seems to be conscious that it must receive some form of energy from either its "I" companion, or else from some other "I," ere it is able to bring into being its mental creations. This consciousness brings with it a realization of an enormous capacity for mental work and creative ability.

But the student soon finds that this is not all that he finds within his inner consciousness. He finds that there exists a mental Something which is able to Will that the "Me" act along certain creative lines, and which is also able to stand aside and witness the mental creation. This part of himself he is taught to call his "I." He is able to rest in its consciousness at will. He finds there not a consciousness of an ability to generate and actively create, in the sense of the gradual process attendant upon mental operations, but rather a sense and consciousness of an ability to project an energy from the "I" to the "Me"—a process of "willing" that the mental creation begin and proceed. He also finds that the "I" is able to stand aside and witness the operations of the "Me's" mental creation and generation. There is this dual aspect in the mind of every person. The "I" represents the Masculine Principle of Mental Gender—the "Me" represents the Female Principle. The "I" represents the Aspect of Being; the "Me" the Aspect of Becoming. You will notice that the Principle of Correspondence operates on this plane just as it does upon the great plane upon which the creation of Universes is performed. The two are similar in kind, although vastly different in degree. "As above, so below; as below, so above."

These aspects of mind—the Masculine and Feminine Principles—the "I" and the "Me"—considered in connection with the well-known mental and psychic phenomena, give the master-key to these dimly known regions of mental operation and manifestation. The principle of Mental Gender gives the truth underlying the whole field of the phenomena of mental influence, etc.

The tendency of the Feminine Principle is always in the direction of receiving impressions, while the tendency of the Masculine Principle is always in the direction of giving out, or expressing. The Feminine Principle has a much more varied field of operation than has the Masculine Principle. The Feminine Principle conducts the work of generating new thoughts, concepts, ideas, including the work of the imagination. The

Masculine Principle contents itself with the work of the "Will," in its varied phases. And yet without the active aid of the Will of the Masculine Principle, the Feminine Principle is apt to rest content with generating mental images which are the result of impressions received from outside, instead of producing original mental creations.

Persons who can give continued attention and thought to a subject actively employ both of the Mental Principles—the Feminine in the work of active mental generation, and the Masculine Will in stimulating and energizing the creative portion of the mind. The majority of persons really employ the Masculine Principle but little, and are content to live according to the thoughts and ideas instilled into the "Me" from the "I" of other minds. But it is not our purpose to dwell upon this phase of the subject, which may be studied from any good text-book upon psychology, with the key that we have given you regarding Mental Gender.

The student of Psychic Phenomena is aware of the wonderful phenomena classified under the head of Telepathy; Thought Transference; Mental Influence; Suggestion; Hypnotism, etc. Many have sought for an explanation of these varied phases of phenomena under the theories of the various "dual mind" teachers. And in a measure they are right, for there is clearly a manifestation of two distinct phases of mental activity. But if such students will consider these "dual minds" in the light of the Hermetic Teachings regarding Vibrations and Mental Gender, they will see that the long sought for key is at hand.

In the phenomena of Telepathy it is seen how the Vibratory Energy of the Masculine Principle is projected toward the Feminine Principle of another person, and the latter takes the seed-thought and allows it to develop into maturity. In the same way Suggestion and Hypnotism operates. The Masculine Principle of the person giving the suggestions directs a steam of Vibratory Energy or Will-Power toward the Feminine Principle of the other person, and the latter accepting it makes it its own and acts and thinks accordingly. An idea thus lodged in the mind of another person grows and develops, and in time is regarded as the rightful mental offspring of the individual, whereas it is in reality like the cuckoo egg placed in the sparrow's nest, where it destroys the rightful offspring and makes itself at home. The normal method is for the Masculine and Feminine Principles in a person's mind to co-ordinate and act harmoniously in conjunction with each other. But, unfortunately, the Masculine Principle in the average person is too lazy to act—the display of Will-Power is too slight—and the consequence is that such persons are ruled almost entirely by the minds and wills of other persons, whom they allow to do their thinking and willing for them. How few original thoughts or original actions are performed by the average person? Are not the majority of persons mere shadows and echoes of others having stronger wills or minds than themselves? The trouble is that the average person dwells almost altogether in his "Me" consciousness, and does not realize that he has such a thing as an "I." He is polarized in his Feminine Principle of Mind, and the Masculine Principle, in which is lodged the Will, is allowed to remain inactive and not employed.

The strong men and women of the world invariably manifest the Masculine Principle of Will, and their strength depends materially upon this fact. Instead of living upon the impressions made upon their minds by others, they dominate their own minds by their Will, obtaining the kind of mental images desired, and moreover dominate the minds of others likewise, in the same manner. Look at the strong people, how they manage to implant their seed-thoughts in the minds of the masses of the people, thus causing the latter to think thoughts in accordance with the desires and wills of the strong individuals. This is why the masses of people are such sheeplike creatures, never originating an idea of their own, nor using their own powers of mental activity.

The manifestation of Mental Gender may be noticed all around us in everyday life. The magnetic persons are those who are able to use the Masculine Principle in the way of impressing their ideas upon others. The actor who makes people weep or cry as he wills, is employing this principle. And so is the successful orator, statesman, preacher, writer or other people who are before the public attention. The peculiar influence exerted by some people over others is due to the manifestation of Mental Gender, along the Vibratorial lines above indicated. In this principle lies the secret of personal magnetism, personal influence, fascination, etc., as well as the phenomena generally grouped under the name of Hypnotism.

The student who has familiarized himself with the phenomena generally spoken of as "psychic" will have discovered the important part played in the said phenomena by that force which science has styled "Suggestion," by which term is meant the process or method whereby an idea is transferred to, or "impressed upon" the mind of another, causing the second mind to act in accordance therewith. A correct understanding of Suggestion is necessary in order to intelligently comprehend the varied psychical phenomena which Suggestion underlies. But, still more is a knowledge of Vibration and Mental Gender necessary for the student of Suggestion. For the whole principle of Suggestion depends upon the principle of Mental Gender and Vibration.

It is customary for the writers and teachers of Suggestion to explain that it is the "objective or voluntary" mind which make the mental impression, or suggestion, upon the "subjective or involuntary" mind. But they do not describe the process or give us any analogy in nature whereby we may more readily comprehend the idea. But if you will think of the matter in the light of the Hermetic Teachings, you will be able to see that the energizing of the Feminine Principle by the Vibratory Energy of the Masculine Principle is in accordance to the universal laws of nature, and that the natural world affords countless analogies whereby the principle may be understood. In fact, the Hermetic Teachings show that the very creation of the Universe follows the same law, and that in all creative manifestations, upon the planes of the spiritual, the mental, and the physical, there is always in operation this principle of Gender—this manifestation of the Masculine and the Feminine Principles. "As above, so below; as below, so above." And more than this, when the principle of Mental Gender is once grasped and understood, the varied phenomena of psychology at once becomes capable of intelligent classification and study, instead of being very much in the dark. The principle "works out" in practice, because it is based upon the immutable universal laws of life.

We shall not enter into an extended discussion of, or description of, the varied phenomena of mental influence or psychic activity. There are many books, many of them quite good, which have been written and published on this subject of late years. The main facts stated in these various books are correct, although the several writers have attempted to explain the phenomena by various pet theories of their own. The student may acquaint himself with these matters, and by using the theory of Mental Gender he will be able to bring order out of the chaos of conflicting theory and teachings, and may, moreover, readily make himself a master of the subject if he be so inclined. The purpose of this work is not to give an extended account of psychic phenomena, but rather to give to the student a master-key whereby he may unlock the many doors leading into the parts of the Temple of Knowledge which he may wish to explore. We feel that in this consideration of the teachings of *The Kybalion*, one may find an explanation which will serve to clear away many perplexing difficulties—a key that will unlock many doors. What is the use of going into detail regarding all of the many features of psychic phenomena and mental science, provided we place in the hands of the student the means whereby he may acquaint himself fully regarding any phase of the subject which may interest him. With the aid of *The Kybalion* one may go through any occult library anew, the old Light from Egypt illuminating many dark pages, and obscure subjects. That is the purpose of this book. We do not come expounding a new philosophy, but rather furnishing the outlines of a great world-old teaching which will make clear the teachings of others—which will serve as a Great Reconciler of differing theories, and opposing doctrines.

15

Hermetic Axioms

"The possession of Knowledge, unless accompanied by a manifestation and expression in Action, is like the hoarding of precious metals—a vain and foolish thing. Knowledge, like Wealth, is intended for Use. The Law of Use is Universal, and he who violates it suffers by reason of his conflict with natural forces."

—THE KYBALION

The Hermetic Teachings, while always having been kept securely locked up in the minds of the fortunate possessors thereof, for reasons which we have already stated, were never intended to be merely stored away and secreted. The Law of Use is dwelt upon in the Teachings, as you may see by reference to the above quotation from *The Kybalion*, which states it forcibly. Knowledge without Use and Expression is a vain thing, bringing no good to its possessor, or to the race. Beware of Mental Miserliness, and express into Action that which you have learned. Study the Axioms and Aphorisms, but practice them also.

We give below some of the more important Hermetic Axioms, from *The Kybalion*, with a few comments added to each. Make these your own, and practice and use them, for they are not really your own until you have Used them.

> "*To change your mood or mental state—change your vibration.*"
>
> —THE KYBALION

One may change his mental vibrations by an effort of Will, in the direction of deliberately fixing the Attention upon a more desirable state. Will directs the Attention, and Attention changes the Vibration. Cultivate the Art of Attention, by means of the Will, and you have solved the secret of the Mastery of Moods and Mental States.

> "*To destroy an undesirable rate of mental vibration, put into operation the Principle of Polarity and concentrate upon the opposite pole to that which you desire to suppress. Kill out the undesirable by changing its polarity.*"
>
> —THE KYBALION

This is one of the most important of the Hermetic Formulas. It is based upon true scientific principles. We have shown you that a mental state and its opposite were merely the two poles of one thing, and that by Mental Transmutation the polarity might be reversed. This principle is known to modern psychologists, who apply it to the breaking up of undesirable habits by bidding their students concentrate upon the opposite quality. If you are possessed of Fear, do not waste time trying to "kill out" Fear, but instead cultivate the quality of Courage, and the Fear

THE BOOK OF HERMETICA

will disappear. Some writers have expressed this idea most forcibly by using the illustration of the dark room. You do not have
to shovel out or sweep out the Darkness, but by merely opening
the shutters and letting in the Light the Darkness has disap-
peared. To kill out a Negative quality, concentrate upon the
Positive Pole of that same quality, and the vibrations will gradually change from Negative to Positive, until finally you will
become polarized on the Positive pole instead of the Negative.
The reverse is also true, as many have found out to their sorrow,
when they have allowed themselves to vibrate too constantly on
the Negative pole of things. By changing your polarity you may
master your moods, change your mental states, remake your
disposition, and build up character. Much of the Mental Mastery
of the advanced Hermetics is due to this application of Polarity,
which is one of the important aspects of Mental Transmutation.
Remember the Hermetic Axiom (quoted previously), which
says:

> "Mind (as well as metals and elements) may be transmuted
> from state to state; degree to degree; condition to condition; pole
> to pole; vibration to vibration."
>
> —THE KYBALION

The mastery of Polarization is the mastery of the fundamental principles of Mental Transmutation or Mental Alchemy, for
unless one acquires the art of changing his own polarity, he will
be unable to affect his environment. An understanding of this
principle will enable one to change his own Polarity, as well as
that of others, if he will but devote the time, care, study and
practice necessary to master the art. The principle is true, but

the results obtained depend upon the persistent patience and practice of the student.

> *"Rhythm may be neutralized by an application of the Art of Polarization."*
>
> —THE KYBALION

As we have explained in previous chapters, the Hermetists hold that the Principle of Rhythm manifests on the Mental Plane as well as on the Physical Plane, and that the bewildering succession of moods, feelings, emotions, and other mental states, are due to the backward and forward swing of the mental pendulum, which carries us from one extreme of feeling to the other. The Hermetists also teach that the Law of Neutralization enables one, to a great extent, to overcome the operation of Rhythm in consciousness. As we have explained, there is a Higher Plane of Consciousness, as well as the ordinary Lower Plane, and the Master by rising mentally to the Higher Plane causes the swing of the mental pendulum to manifest on the Lower Plane, and he, dwelling on his Higher Plane, escapes the consciousness of the swing backward. This is effected by polarizing on the Higher Self, and thus raising the mental vibrations of the Ego above those of the ordinary plane of consciousness. It is akin to rising above a thing, and allowing it to pass beneath you. The advanced Hermetist polarizes himself at the Positive Pole of his Being—the "I Am" pole rather than the pole of personality, and by "refusing" and "denying" the operation of Rhythm, raises himself above its plane of consciousness, and standing firm in his Statement of Being he allows the pendulum to swing back on the Lower Plane without changing his Polarity. This is accomplished by all individuals who have attained any degree of self-mastery, whether they understand the law or not. Such persons simply "refuse" to allow themselves to be swung back by the pendulum of mood and emotion, and by steadfastly affirming the superiority, they remain polarized on the Positive pole. The Master, of course, attains a far greater degree of proficiency, because he understands the law which he is overcoming by a higher law, and by the use of his Will he attains a degree of Poise and Mental Steadfastness almost impossible of belief on the part of those who allow themselves to be swung backward and forward by the mental pendulum of moods and feelings.

Remember, always, however, that you do not really destroy the Principle of Rhythm, for that is indestructible. You simply overcome one law by counter-balancing it with another, and thus maintain an equilibrium. The laws of balance and counter-balance are in operation on the mental as well as on the physical planes, and an understanding of these laws enables one to seem to overthrow laws, whereas he is merely exerting a counterbalance.

> "Nothing escapes the Principle of Cause and Effect, but there are many Planes of Causation, and one may use the laws of the higher to overcome the laws of the lower."
>
> —THE KYBALION

By an understanding of the practice of Polarization, the Hermetists rise to a higher plane of Causation and thus counterbalance the laws of the lower planes of Causation. By rising above the plane of ordinary Causes they become themselves, in a degree, Causes instead of being merely Caused. By being able to master their own moods and feelings, and by being able to neutralize Rhythm, as we have already explained, they are able to escape a great part of the operations of Cause and Effect on the ordinary plane. The masses of people are carried along, obedient to their environment; the wills and desires of others stronger than themselves; the effects of inherited tendencies; the suggestions of those about them; and other outward causes; which tend to move them about on the chess-board of life like mere pawns. By rising above these influencing causes, the advanced Hermetists seek a higher plane of mental action, and by dominating their moods, emotions, impulses and feelings, they create for themselves new characters, qualities and powers, by which they overcome their ordinary environment, and thus become practically players instead of mere Pawns. Such people help to play the game of life understandingly, instead of being moved about this way and that way by stronger influences and powers and wills. They use the Principle of Cause and Effect, instead of being used by it. Of course, even the highest are subject to the Principle as it manifests on the higher planes, but on the lower planes of activity, they are Masters instead of Slaves. As *The Kybalion* says:

> "*The wise ones serve on the higher, but rule on the lower. They obey the laws coming from above them, but on their own plane, and those below them, they rule and give orders. And, yet, in so doing, they form a part of the Principle, instead of opposing it. The wise man falls in with the Law, and by understanding its movements he operates it instead of being its blind slave. Just as does the skilled swimmer turn this way and that way, going and coming as he will, instead of being as the log which is carried here and there—so is the wise man as compared to*

the ordinary man—and yet both swimmer and log; wise man
and fool, are subject to Law. He who understands this is well
on the road to Mastery."

—THE KYBALION

In conclusion let us again call your attention to the Hermetic
Axiom:

"True Hermetic Transmutation is a Mental Art."

—THE KYBALION

In the above axiom, the Hermetists teach that the great work
of influencing one's environment is accomplished by Mental
Power. The Universe being wholly mental, it follows that it may
be ruled only by Mentality. And in this truth is to be found an
explanation of all the phenomena and manifestations of the various mental powers which are attracting so much attention and
study in these earlier years of the Twentieth Century. Back of
and under the teachings of the various cults and schools, remains
ever constant the principle of the Mental Substance of the Universe. If the Universe be Mental in its substantial nature, then it
follows that Mental Transmutation must change the conditions
and phenomena of the Universe. If the Universe is Mental, then
Mind must be the highest power affecting its phenomena. If this
be understood then all the so-called "miracles" and "wonder-
workings" are seen plainly for what they are.

"THE ALL is MIND; The Universe is Mental."

—THE KYBALION